LECTURE 1

Giving these talks is a stimulating assignment for me, because young people attracted to the Trotskyist program show a salutary interest in all aspects of the history of our movement. This quality enables young people to learn today from past class struggle experience. No less important, it helps to avoid repetition of old mistakes. In general, young rebels are able to stand on the shoulders of their predecessors in going forward to meet today's revolutionary tasks.

Interest in the history of the Socialist Workers Party has centered on the political side. The political line is the key to a correct revolutionary outlook, and literature on political history is more readily available. The connection between organizational methods and political outlook is not readily apparent. It takes time and experience to grasp the interrelationship between the two, and literature on the organizational question itself is less readily available.

For these reasons, the present talks should serve a general need, and I will undertake in these discussions, to summarize the main lines of the Socialist Workers Party's organizational history. I will undertake to sketch an overall picture and offer some guides to further study of the subject.

It's best to begin with the relationship of organizational conceptions to the political aims of the movement. The organizational structure must derive from the political objectives it is designed to serve. That is paramount. Given a correct program, then organizational strength becomes vital to success. But size alone is a false criterion for the strength of an organization. The question remains: can it meet the test of class struggle reality? History shows that the party program is the key to the answer. Without a correct program, an organization is built of political straw, and it will inevitably collapse in the winds of social conflict.

I would cite as a case in point the rise and decline of the so-called New Left of modern times. This was a get-rich-quick scheme. They were going to show the so-called "old left" how to do it. Their basic approach was first, to get organized, and then to develop a political program. "We'll figure out something," they said, "we'll get the show on the road." Toward this end, they evolved what they described as the method of "participatory democracy," that is, anybody who stepped up could pose as a leader. This method opened the way for angle merchants to become dominant in the leading circles of the New Left. These were comprised mainly of factional sharpies and personally ambitious political ignoramuses with big mouths. This gang misled the young rebels who were attracted to the New Left into a variety of political escapades ranging from ultraleft adventurism to new forms of sorties into the old game of capitalist politics. The whole process resulted in the political discreditment of the New Left and its organizational disintegration.

The fate of the New Left was no surprise to experienced revolutionists. Its so-called "participatory democracy" was nothing more than a long-known concept that has gone by the name of political all-inclusiveness. It is an old concept, and it was long ago refuted by experience. Now I want to point out that the concept of political all-inclusiveness, as we are discussing it here, has nothing to do with the question of non-exclusion in uniting a broad formation around a single issue as, for instance, in the antiwar movement where people of differing political views come together on one common agreed-upon aim, in this case, mass action against the war. When you speak of political all-inclusiveness, as implied in the concept of "participatory democracy," you are not talking about organizing a united front around a single issue. You're talking about the question of building a political party. And that is altogether different.

I will return later to this subject of all-inclusiveness in describing to you some of the aspects of the history of the SWP on the organizational question. But as for the New Left experience, it proves once more that organizational forms cannot be devised independently of politics. To be viable, an organization must be based on defined political objectives. Politics then determines the kind of organization that is needed, and the specific form that organization must take.

The Socialist Workers Party's structure and its organizational principles derive from the party's political outlook. We perceive an objective trend towards deepening social crisis and sharpening class conflict. That is our political point of departure. As that process continues to unfold it will make imperative a revolutionary solution of the basic social problems afflicting the peoples of this country and of the world. In anticipation of such developments in the United States, and in active preparation for those developments, we have reached a determination as to the kind of a party our movement should set out to build.

The SWP's central aim is set forth in our program of abolishing capitalism and reorganizing the United States on a socialist basis. We recognize that in this endeavor, we are up against the most powerful and ruthless ruling class in the history of the world. From that, it follows that the revolutionary party must be constructed as a cohesive and disciplined combat organization. That is why the Socialist Workers Party has sought to base itself on the tested and proven Leninist rules of organization. These can be summed up in the concept of democratic centralism. Defined in a broad generalization, democratic centralism constitutes an interrelated process of democracy in deciding party policy, and centralized action in carrying it out.

While we're stating the basic aspects, let us turn to a second generalization that follows, concerning attacks on democratic centralism. Such attacks stem primarily from false definitions of democracy. Despite the claims of windbags, democracy does not imply endless talk; nor is it a license for undisciplined organizational conduct, as factional hooligans will try to tell you. Democracy is basically a method of reaching a decision. It requires that first all viewpoints be heard in debating a question, then a vote is taken, and then the time has come for action. That is where centralism takes over. Centralism is based on the democratic principle of majority rule. It stems from the concept of making a decision by majority vote. Basically, it is a method of exercising the right of the majority to see that its decision is carried out.

Under democratic centralist procedures, after a decision has been made in a dispute, those in the minority are bound by the party decision reached by majority vote. All party members are required to help carry out the party decision. Authority becomes centralized through the official party bodies, and the party confronts the outside world with a single policy, that of the majority. A dissident minority is not asked to give up its views. It must simply await an appropriate time to raise the disputed issues inside the party again. And comrades in a minority are given an unqualified opportunity to serve the party in every respect in the party's daily life.

In determining the interplay of democracy and centralism on a working basis, the party, as a whole, has rights based on the principle of majority rule. The party as a whole determines the form and limits of internal discussion in the organization at each juncture. This is done in order to ensure that party work is not disrupted and disorganized. Official bodies in the party may organize a discussion at any time, and in whatever form the situation requires.

Let me give you a recent example. Ordinarily, at a party convention, when a vote is taken on basic resolutions, that settles the line and ends the discussion for the next immediate period. But, at the party convention in 1969 the convention authorized a continuation of internal discussion of the political resolution. There were two reasons for this. First, it was not a conjunctural political resolution; it was a draft that undertook to review quite a substantial past period of the history of political evolution in this country, and to project our long-range perspectives for the period ahead. Second, just as we were nearing the convention, there was a sudden—you could almost say qualitative—advance in the development of the Chicano struggle and the women's liberation movement.

Now in the resolution these questions had not had adequate attention commensurate with the obvious needs of the changing situation, so the convention authorized the continuation of a literary discussion on the political resolution for a few months afterwards. This was held, and then a final decision was made on the general line of the resolution at a plenum of the National Committee in the spring of 1970. That terminated the discussion for the present time. Now I might say that this is not ordinary, but it is a good way to illustrate that there is nothing rigid, mechanical, or dogmatic about the attempts of the party to work out in living experience the interplay between democracy and centralism, between discussion and action.

I mentioned that it was a literary discussion. That meant that the subject was open for comment by all party members in an internal discussion bulletin. But the party did not provide for oral discussion in the party branches. In this way party work proceeded on the basis of the general convention decisions, and those who had further thoughts to contribute on these particular aspects of the political resolution could do so in writing. Comrades then had a chance to think about these questions before the plenum where we made the final decision.

I will cite a second, very basic example concerning discussion that is explicitly provided in the constitution of the party. Prior to a national convention, which by direction of the constitution must be held at least every two years, a national discussion must be organized within the party. That discussion takes place in both literary form, in the bulletin, and in oral form, in discussion in the party branches, during the preconvention discussion period, which is set for two to four months, depending on the given situation. And during that preconvention discussion, any member of the party can raise any question for consideration by the party. In this way, we attain another aspect of the equilibrium between democracy and centralism, discussion and action. People aren't allowed to talk all the time, no matter what season it is, just because they've got a lot of oil in the joints of their jaws; but at the same time, provision is made at reasonable frequency to enable anyone in the party to bring up any question in order to be sure we're keeping things on an even keel.

To see how democratic centralism is operative, we should look at it from another aspect as well. It requires political cohesiveness inside the party, which derives from relative political homogeneity in the party ranks. There is homogeneity in the sense of fundamental agreement with the party's program and principles; and this, in turn, lays the foundation for the application of discipline, which has to be a voluntary matter in the party; and discipline, in turn, permits united action with a common purpose. Within the framework of basic political homogeneity, the party provides ample room for political differences. There is a free and democratic internal atmosphere prevalent in the party. Full opportunity exists for the expression of dissident views. The right to organize tendencies and factions around one or another viewpoint inside the party is safeguarded. On this basis, given the necessary sense of party loyalty, comrades can argue out questions on the basis of principles, and they are able to act from the standpoint of principles. Through this approach, to the degree that it is attained, political differences can be resolved democratically, the party can maintain its internal stability, its policies can be carried out in a centralized manner, and it is able to correct mistakes it may make without disruption or internal convulsion.

Now, I have undertaken to state rather abstractly the essentials of the Leninist concept, but democratic centralism does not wholly lend itself to schematic definition. In the last analysis, it has to be worked out in life. The interplay between democracy in deciding policy and centralism in carrying it out comes to equilibrium inside a living movement in the course of the tests and experiences through which it passes. This consideration requires that we now pass from an abstract delineation of the Leninist concept to the SWP's development of its organizational principles as an integral part of the living history of the party. (Everything I have said up to now has been more or less a preamble to discussing the main lines of the actual historical development of our organizational principles.)

The party's first resolution on the organizational question, undertaking to codify its principles, was adopted by the founding convention of the Socialist Workers Party in 1938. That convention culminated ten years' party building work. The effort had begun initially through the Trotskyist cadres that were expelled from the Communist Party in 1928. These cadres were reinforced during the radicalization of the 1930's through individual recruitment of worker and student militants. The first major new acquisition, in bloc, came in 1934 through the fusion of the Trotskyist organization (then known as the Communist League of America) with the American Workers Party, a body of militant young workers and students who were moving in the same basic political direction, but who had had a separate organizational form. These two movements fused in 1934 to form what was then known as the Workers Party. Then, in the spring of 1936, this fused movement entered the Socialist Party for the purpose of getting into direct contact with the Socialist Party's left wing, which was in many respects the counterpart of the radicalizing young militants that had gathered around the American Workers Party at an earlier period. This leftwing formation, now comprised of the previous leftwing SP militants and the Trotskyists who had entered the Socialist Party, was expelled from that organization in 1937. These, in brief, were the forces that came together at the beginning of 1938, constituting the founding cadres of the SWP.

The 1938 organizational resolution adopted at the founding convention had a dual purpose. One aim was to set down the party's organizational concepts in line with the revolutionary principles embodied in the program of the founding convention. The second aim was to cement the fusion with the leftwing splitoff from the Socialist Party by clarifying the Leninist views on party organization. In this respect, Leninist principles were counterposed to both Stalinist and social-democratic organizational methods.

The founding cadres of Trotskyism had their own firsthand experience with Stalinism in the process of being thrown out of the Communist Party. When the Stalin-Trotsky split developed, you did not have to declare for Trotsky as against Stalin to be thrown out. All you had to do was stand up and ask why Trotsky was thrown out in Russia and you were expelled from the Communist Party in this country. But you didn't have to do even that. If some other member of the party got thrown out on the grounds that he or she was a Trotskyist, and you took the floor to ask why he or she was thrown out, you, too, were out. Just like that. It was, to use the modern terminology—it was instant expulsion. And this process on the part of the Stalinists epitomized the general character of Stalinist monolithism, which is the suppression of internal political dissent, the proscription of the organization of tendencies and factions, and the imposition of rigid political conformity by a dictatorial official regime. The resolution adopted in 1938 carefully provided that there be no traces of these procedures in our party.

Our other experience was with the bureaucratic hacks in the Socialist Party. They pretended to practice political all-inclusiveness. (Now we have come back to that question from a slightly different point of view. This was the original critter.) As the Socialist Party formally projected it, all who considered themselves socialists should get together in one party, with equal rights for all. It turned out, however, that some inside the party were more equal than others. At a convention of the Socialist Party, they would allow discussion from the floor, members could come as delegates from their branches and get up and pop off as they wished. It might seem that everything was decided democratically. But it was not so at all. All the time the self-perpetuating leadership of top bureaucratic hacks were making horse trades and deals with one another behind the scenes to settle policy, to decide who would remain in office, who would get this post, who would get that post. It was a fake and a fraud. You have had a somewhat comparable experience in the antiwar movement today, with the types who oppose the holding of representative national antiwar conferences to decide policy democratically and instead want to have decisions made behind the scenes in star chamber commissions by self-appointed leaders. I don't think I need to name any names, you all know the types.

There was another aspect to the operation of so-called political all-inclusiveness in the social democratic form. The bureaucratic regime in the organization hounded the revolutionary militants, suppressed their rights, and took every opportunity to throw them out of the organization. And, at the same time, this regime allowed the rightwing scoundrels in the organization to commit the worst political crimes in the name of the party. The 1938 resolution of the SWP made sure that there would be no repetition of those procedures with respect to our party. The resolution specifically rejected so-called political all-inclusiveness as the sham and fraud that it was. It declared the SWP inclusive only in the sense that the party accepts into its ranks those who accept its program; admission is denied to those who reject its program—politics first, politics only, being the criteria.

Now experience with the social democratic proclivities to make a mockery of the party led to another provision in the 1938 SWP document. That document stipulates that membership in the Socialist Workers Party implies the obligation of 100% loyalty to the organization. No free lancers, no peddlers of their own quack political medicine are allowed to speak in the name of the SWP. And this demand of loyalty stressed in the resolution also means rejection from party ranks of all agents of hostile groups, and intolerance of divided loyalties. I want to emphasize this point, because in the next talk we're going to discuss an internal conflict within the SWP where this question was very much in the fore.

As a reflex against Stalinist and social democratic bureaucratism, the 1938 resolution put heavy emphasis on the rights of the party rank and file. It stressed the value to the party of a self-acting and critical-minded membership. The fundamental rights of the membership were explicitly stated. These included freedom of discussion, debate and criticism inside the party, in accordance with procedures decided by the party. Another explicit right is that of being democratically represented at policy-making assemblies of the party. Still another is the right of the membership to have a final and decisive vote in determining the program, policies and leadership of the party.

The resolution also gave attention to the problem of windbags, who seem to turn up in all seasons and from all quarters. The party, it stressed, is not a discussion club. It does not debate endlessly without reaching a binding decision that leads to action. The rights of individual members do not contravene the rights of the party as a whole. Party democracy means not only the protection of the rights of a minority, but also protection of the rule of the majority. Convention decisions are binding on all party members without exception, and any member who violates the decisions of the convention, the resolution asserted, or who attempts to revive discussion of decided questions without the formal authorization of the party, forfeits his or her right to membership in the organization.

The resolution also dealt with the futility of trying to carry out revolutionary activity with a heterogeneous, undisciplined, untrained organization. It stressed the need for centralized direction of party work, and affirmed this as a prerequisite for sustained and disciplined political action. Distinct powers were accorded to the party's National Committee. These include: authority to act in the name of the party between conventions, and to supervise, coordinate and direct all the party's activities.

On the leadership question, a lesson was drawn from an old mistake once made by the IWW, which at one time required that a leader holding an official post in the IWW had to return to the ranks after a single term in office. A leader could not be reelected. This practice was conceived as a safeguard against bureaucratism. What it led to, in fact, was the disruption of stability and continuity in leadership. The resolution pointed out that sustained party activity presupposes continuity of leadership. This can be attained on a sound basis through cadres that have come up through the ranks because of demonstrated leadership ability; that is, in the eyes of the rank and file they have earned the votes to be elected as leaders. And their election to leadership affords a preliminary test of their endurance and trustworthiness. From this evolves a process of selection, through which leadership ability and continuity can be maintained. Continuity in leadership, it was stressed, does not signify a self-perpetuating leadership. The warrant for leadership trust must be continuously proven before the party ranks.

To illustrate this point, I will cite an experience back in 1942, in the very early stages of the dispute that developed with the Morrow-Goldman faction inside the party. Morrow came into the convention—he was a member of the National Committee, the editor of the paper, a leader of some stature in the party at that time—he came up with the proposition that members of the National Committee could be removed from the National Committee only for cause. The party reacted strongly against this idea and any notion of the kind was explicitly ruled out when the concepts for the functioning of the nominating commission were formally established by the 1944 party convention. Leaders are to remain on the National Committee only for cause. That basic concept is carried out to a much more precise degree in the present, very important function of selection of the National Committee by the party convention. Our practice is to have a nominating commission, selected from among the convention delegates by the delegates. It is a representative commission, representative of the party as a whole, sort of a microcosm of the convention itself. This commission considers the list of the members of the outgoing National Committee, and it also has before it nominations to the Committee which have been submitted by various delegates or delegations. It examines the lists, discusses the names, and decides what kind of recommendations to make to the convention. These recommendations are then presented to the convention delegates who make the final decision by a democratic vote. Usually one of the very first actions of the nominating commission is to sit down and examine the names on the outgoing National Committee. They don't say, "Has somebody a reason why such-and-such a person can't stay on the National Committee?" That's not the way they start at all. For each name the question asked is, "Is there anybody who would like to discuss the question of this comrade remaining on the Committee before we make a decision?" If somebody wants to discuss it, then that name is held over. The commission first decides which of the outgoing members of the National Committee everybody seems to feel ought to remain, and then takes up the others. There's no self-perpetuation in the leadership at all.

Now, let's look at it from another point of view. A periodic appraisal is necessary in order to make readjustments, from time to time, in the leadership, and make it possible for the party to carry forward in the best possible way. This procedure safeguards the party against the development of dry rot in its official bodies; helps to keep it alive, dynamic, in touch with the times. Conflicts between the older and younger elements in the party are minimized by this carefully conducted process of adjustment and readjustment in the structure of the leadership. And bureaucratic remoteness from the real life of the party among the leaders is prevented.

These, as I have sought to review here, are some basic forms of the application of democratic centralism as they evolved out of the first ten years of the experience of the Trotskyist movement. They laid a foundation for carrying the movement forward in its work on the basis of Leninist principles. They represent both an application of the basic organizational concepts of Lenin and a rejection of the experience in the Communist Party and the Socialist Party, and set the stage for the Trotskyist party in this country to begin its own experience, which contains some very rich lessons. Tomorrow we will begin a review of the subsequent history of disputes within the SWP on the question of organizational principles.

LECTURE 2

Like all social formations, a revolutionary party is subject to external influences and internal change. Alien class pressures bear down upon the party in a hostile political environment. At times this generates dissident political moods in the ranks of the organization that lead to a challenge of some aspect of the party's program. When that happens, the relationship between organization and politics becomes very plain. The internal discussion that ensues reveals that a rift has developed in the party's political homogeneity. And from that, an attack usually follows on the principle of majority rule, taking the form of demands for special minority rights. Political dissidents tend to develop an urge to violate democratic centralism and to debase the party norms. As a consequence, organizational differences become a corollary of a sharp political dispute inside the party.

In the history of the Socialist Workers Party, such demands for special minority rights have fallen into three general categories: 1.) minority demands that it be allowed to carry out its own line publicly; 2.) minority attempts to veto the implementation of majority policy; 3.) opposition to majority control over minority conduct inside the party. Each of these general types of organizational demands by dissident minorities have arisen at different stages in the party's history.

The first came up in 1939–40 during an internal party crisis following the signing of the Stalin-Hitler pact in 1939, on the eve of Germany's invasion of Poland and the opening of the second World War. A petty bourgeois wing within the party, led by Burnham, Shachtman, and Abern capitulated in that situation to the pressures of bourgeois public opinion, particularly the scandalization of the Soviet Union that was being pressed vigorously by the bourgeois propaganda media after the signing of the Stalin-Hitler pact. What was so deadly serious about the internal party conflict was that this petty bourgeois opposition renounced the Trotskyist position of unconditional defense of the Soviet Union against imperialist attack. That was a mighty serious political matter as World War II was beginning. This shift in political line led the minority to demand that it be allowed to publish its own public organ in which it would promulgate its line to the world at large. A debate on the organization question ensued that lasted up to the convention in April, 1940 where the petty bourgeois opposition split from the party. The basic material dealing with the organizational side of this dispute in 1939 and 1940 is very well covered in a book by Comrade James P. Cannon entitled *The Struggle for a Proletarian Party*. I recommend it for your careful attention and study.

In the aftermath of this fight at the convention in 1940 the party adopted a supplement to the 1938 resolution on the party's organizational principles. The new document reaffirmed the general line of the 1938 draft that we discussed yesterday. It also brought the party's statement of organizational principles up to date in the light of the experience with the Burnham-Shachtman-Abern opposition of 1939–40.

To give you the highlights of the additions made in the 1940 resolution, let me begin as follows. During the preconvention discussion at that time, the Burnhamites within the petty bourgeois opposition echoed the social democratic line that Stalinism is the natural end product of Bolshevism. The 1940 resolution explicitly and categorically rejected this false thesis. It emphasized, rather, that the Socialist Workers Party models its organizational forms and methods after those of the Russian Bolsheviks, simply adapting them to concrete political conditions within this country.

On a second matter, the minority demands for an independent public organ were rejected by the convention and the resolution dealt with this matter as well. Such an organ, it was pointed out, would expound a program in opposition to that of the party majority. That would mean, in effect, freeing the minority from party control over its public activities, and such a step would represent a definitive abandonment of the Leninist principles of democratic centralism. The party press, the resolution stated, is the central medium for expression of the party line. Control of the press must be lodged directly in the hands of the National Committee of the party, as elected by a party convention. The editors of the press must loyally interpret the party line in its pages. It was pointed out that the party may decide to open the press to a public discussion on a given occasion, but that is a matter for the party to decide and not something that a minority can demand as a right.

Let me give you an example of such a public discussion. This occurred quite recently—in the period prior to the 1969 convention. You will recall that the draft resolution setting forth a transitional program for the Black liberation struggle was published in *The Militant,* not just in an internal discussion bulletin. And discussion in the columns of *The Militant* was invited. There were two reasons for this decision. First, so far as the party itself was concerned, it was clear that there was an essentially homogeneous view within the party on the subject matter of the resolution. Clearly there would be no fierce debate within the party. In such a discussion it was not a question of the paper projecting two different programs from within the party. Secondly, inviting public discussion of this program would help the party communicate its thinking on the developing stages of the Black liberation struggle to organizations in the Black movement. It would help to get them familiar with our ideas and improve our relations with them. It would enhance our influence among Black organizations and our potential for winning recruits to the party from among them. On these two bases, it was considered both advisable and possible that there be a public discussion of the question on that particular occasion. Now, I stress that this procedure is a matter for the party to decide. It is not a matter where a minority can purport to exercise any right it may fancy it has to a public discussion of disputed questions in the party. And in no case, the resolution made crystal clear, can the discussion be made one in which diametrically opposite programs emanate publicly from within the party.

Another category taken up in the 1940 resolution was the question of clique formations. The resolution specifically condemned the Abern clique, which was a part of the 1939–40 petty bourgeois opposition. The clique was characterized in the resolution as an unprincipled combination based on personal loyalties rather than political agreement. It was described as seeking rewards within the party for those whose primary loyalty was to the clique.

In our final session we will return to the question of cliques in a different context, in a later internal development within the party, but before I pass to the next point, I want to call to your attention two items that are worth study here. There is a specific section dealing with the Abern clique in Comrade Cannon's book, *The Struggle for a Proletarian Party.* If you want to learn about cliques, what kind of an animal a clique is, how it operates, what its feeding habits are, what its forms of entertainment are, and other basic zoological information you will get a good idea from this section of Comrade Cannon's book. There is a second valuable item that appeared in the 1940 fight. It was an article by Joe Hansen, entitled "The Abern Clique." It has not yet been republished, but it is in the files of the party's internal material. It is kind of a John Gunther type account, you know, "Inside the Abern Clique," and you will find it very informative and educational in a number of ways.

Coming now to other aspects of the 1940 resolution, note was taken of the emphasis in the 1938 resolution on the democratic aspects of democratic centralism, particularly the stress on the right of party membership as against arrogant leaders with a bureaucratic bent. Recall our discussion of that point yesterday. The resolution of 1940 affirmed that the democratic rights of the party membership are faithfully preserved, just as they were delineated in the previous resolution, and that the widest latitude of discussion is given to all dissenting groups and individuals in the party. Attention was also called, in the 1940 document, to the conditions of the pending entry of the United States into World War II, which confronted us with some very specific and difficult problems at that particular conjuncture in history. These circumstances made it necessary for the party to tighten up its activities. The organizational structure needed to be more firmly centralized. A maximum of membership activity was to be required, and there had to be a strict adherence to party discipline. Cognizance was taken of the way the petty bourgeois opposition had proven to be a transmission belt for alien class influence in the 1939–40 experience, and with the country heading toward war, this circumstance called for strong emphasis on efforts to proletarianize the party. A series of steps were outlined in the resolution calculated to root the party more deeply in the trade union and the working class neighborhoods. Major efforts were called for to recruit worker militants into the party as we headed toward World War II.

One of the objective premises for this emphasis in the 1940 resolution was the contrasting composition of the majority and the minority in the fight over unconditional defense of the Soviet Union against imperialist attack, which had been a central issue in the political conflict. The majority was a little over 50% and the minority was something over 40%—it was a hairline split, a deep one. In composition, the overwhelming bulk of the members of the majority were workers, with a few students and intellectuals going along with them. The overwhelming bulk of the minority were petty bourgeois in composition—primarily students and intellectuals of one or another type, with a random worker here and there who had gone along with them. So to all practical intents and purposes the split was essentially a parting of the two diverse categories of class composition within the party as we went into World War II.

The conduct of the petty bourgeois opposition took the form of a disdain for the party, a sneering, contemptuous attitude. I remember when Comrade Cannon was reporting on the organization question at the 1940 convention, where the split came. He was trying to talk, and he was being heckled by the minority. And he turned to them—they had segregated themselves over in one side of the convention hall—and he said, "If the giggling caucus will just bear with me for this one last speech, I will be forever grateful." This characterized the whole attitude of the minority.

Perhaps I can define that minority attitude further by indicating some of the things that were explicitly stated in the 1940 resolution. It said that to cleanse the party from the attitudes manifested by the minority, the party must be rid of any discussion club atmosphere inside its ranks. There must not be an irresponsible attitude toward assignments given to comrades by the party. Cynical and smart aleck disrespect for the party had to be rooted out. In proscribing these attitudes within the party, the resolution was also describing exactly what the conduct of the petty bourgeois opposition had become.

The resolution called for efforts to bring more workers into leading party committees, and a provision was inserted proscribing student youth from going directly onto the National Committee of the party. It was stipulated that students must first serve an apprenticeship in the workers movement. That provision was later changed, as I will describe in our session tomorrow. I want to note it for your attention here to make clear to you one of the conjunctural steps that was taken by the party under the objective conditions of the country's pending entry into World War II, in the face of the experience we had had with this petty bourgeois opposition.

Some other general prerequisites for membership on the National Committee were also laid down in the resolution. These were designed to deal with attitudes that were manifested by National Committee members who were leaders of the petty bourgeois opposition.

Just let me cite one example. A very serious problem had arisen which made it necessary for some of the leading members on the National Committee out in the field to be called into the center for a special consultation. One of them was Ray Dunne, who had more than a few things to do in Minneapolis. Another was Al Goldman, who was busy in Chicago. I was the third one—I was an organizer for the Teamsters at that time, and happened to be in the middle of a strike in Dallas, Texas. But we all dropped everything and went to New York for a special meeting with the Political Committee. And when we got there we had to sit and cool our heels for two hours while

James Burnham finished a little bridge session that his wife had arranged for that afternoon. Well, this describes an awful lot. I just happened to be visiting New York another time when there was a social, and I saw another one of them drop by on the evening of the party social dressed in tails and white tie. He was on his way to some swank affair, but he came by to slum for a few minutes with the comrades on his way. So the resolution had a little something to say about its attitude toward what was expected of National Committee members.

It stated that candidates for the National Committee had to be ready to subordinate their personal life to the needs of the party. That stands. They must be prepared to devote full time to the party, upon the demand of the National Committee. I remember that some of these leaders of that 1939–1940 opposition had their own angles or vocations, and the party was a kind of an avocation. They made adequate livings at their vocations. But if there was a financial crisis in the party, the first thing these jokers would think of was to hold up the party payroll. The party payroll was composed of a few comrades receiving just enough to get by, and these petty bourgeois types displayed an absolutely cavalier attitude toward them. The party full-timers were people giving everything they've got to the party on a day-by-day basis, asking no more than that the party be humane enough to help them keep alive while they do their work. So this stipulation in the 1940 resolution not only expected National Committee members to be sensitive to the needs of the comrades who are working full time for the party for peanuts, but required that they be prepared to do it themselves, if the party asked it of them. If they weren't prepared to do that, they weren't caliber enough to be considered a member of the National Committee of the party, they didn't quite measure up to some of the minimum expectations the party has the right to ask of its leaders.

A third provision of the resolution was that candidates for the National Committee must have demonstrated firmness of character and unconditional loyalty to the party. This harks back to the discussion we were having about the importance of leadership in the party and the stakes that the party puts in the leadership under a given set of combat conditions.

Now with these additions, which cover the main lines of change in the 1940 resolution as compared with 1938, the party's statement of its organizational principles remained unchanged until the 1950's.

We had some internal struggles in that period. There was the fight in the mid-1940's with the Goldman-Morrow opposition. There was the case of the Johnsonites who went out very shortly after the Korean war opened in the midst of the developing witch hunt. The Johnsonites were a state capitalist tendency. In my opinion they just had so many differences with the party that they didn't see any percentage in remaining in a party that was going to be subject to all the harassments and persecutions of the witch hunt, and under conditions of war. So they walked out. They set a timetable and did it in a very well-organized way.

But in the cases of the Johnsonites and the Goldman-Morrow minority, nothing evolved that required any additions to the party's organizational principles. So I will pass over these and some other internal disputes that developed, because in going back over the history of internal struggles in the party, I am dealing only with those that resulted in written additions and modifications to the party's basic statement of its organizational principles.

The next of these struggles occurred in the 1950's. In 1952 a major internal party conflict that had been gestating for a period of about five years erupted in full blast. It stemmed from the reactionary political atmosphere of the time. Years of cold war and witch hunting had brought on a military intervention in Korea by US imperialists and the rise of McCarthyism here at home. And this adverse objective situation began to have repercussions inside the ranks of the SWP. A minority faction developed under the leadership of Bert Cochran. Politically, it was characterized by loss of faith in the working class. The minority saw no chance of building a revolutionary party strong enough to smash the bureaucratic obstacles within the labor movement and lead the masses to the conquest of power. And when I speak of the labor movement here, I'm referring to everything from the bureaucracies in the unions in the United States to the bureaucratic gang in Moscow. The Cochranites turned to opportunist adaptation, to the concept of self-reform of the bureaucracies.

They began to look upon the party's program as an obstacle to their changed political course.

Organizationally, the Cochran faction sought to exercise veto powers within the official party bodies. They focused particularly on the Political Committee of the party. The Political Committee is an executive sub-body of the National Committee, elected by the National Committee. Just as the National Committee looks to the administering of party affairs between party conventions, the Political Committee looks to the administering of party affairs between plenums of the National Committee. This was the body in which the Cochranites put their focus.

In the Political Committee they would demand that a poll, a referendum vote be taken of the National Committee when a decision was made in the Political Committee with which they had strong objection. Their intent was to impose dual leadership authority, and thereby obstruct the carrying out of official party policy. And this too was a direct attack on the principle of majority rule.

The dispute with the Cochranites led to adoption of a new organizational document by the May 1953 plenum of the National Committee. It reaffirmed the general line of the 1938 and 1940 resolutions, and at the same time added new provisions based on the experience with the Cochranites. In rejecting the minority demand for dual leadership authority, the 1953 resolution called attention to the authority invested in the National Committee by the party constitution. It states that the National Committee directs the party's work and decides questions of policy between conventions in accordance with the convention decisions. The National Committee appoints subordinate officers and subcommittees, including the Political Committee, and between conventions, the National Committee constitutes the central authority of the party.

The resolution also set forth the powers of the Political Committee. Between National Committee plenums, the resolution states, the Political Committee functions as the central political-administrative authority of the party, acting in the name of the National Committee. All party units and individual party members are required to comply with the directives of the Political Committee. They have the right to appeal such directives to a plenum of the National Committee, but an appeal can't be used as an interim veto of a Political Committee decision. If you allowed that, you'd be right back where you were with the Cochranites, who tried to paralyze the Political Committee with demands for referendum polls of the National Committee. The resolution made it optional with the Political Committee to decide whether or not it would poll the National Committee on a given question.

Sometimes the Political Committee might find it advisable to do so. Let me give you an example. When the 1968 presidential campaign was being prepared, and the question of recommending the presidential ticket was before the Political Committee, we wanted to have a pretty good tentative idea of the reaction of the party as a whole to the recommendations on the ticket. Since both the candidates we had in mind were very active in many important spheres of work, it required some organizational readjustments to free them for the activities of the presidential campaign. For these reasons, before it took more formal steps, the Political Committee felt it advisable to take a consultative poll of the National Committee with its recommendations on the ticket to be proposed to the party. With the National Committee in complete agreement with the recommendation, we went on from there, and the party ratified the nomination of Halstead and Boutelle as the ticket. This is an example of how under certain circumstances it's in the best interests of the organization for the Political Committee to take such a step.

But the object of the 1953 provision was to make it clear that a PC minority can't force the PC to poll the NC as a method of putting a stop order on the carrying out of a PC decision. There is only one circumstance under which the resolution made a poll of the National Committee mandatory: a poll must be taken if any National Committee member requests the calling of a plenum. The PC is required to comply with the majority decision of the NC in such a poll. That latter provision helps to make clear how meticulously careful the party is in not throwing out of balance the interrelation between democracy and centralism, at the same time that it is paying scrupulous attention to the needs of carrying out centralized action after the party has made a decision. If the PC didn't have to take a poll of the NC under any circumstances, it is conceivable that a given PC, for whatever reasons, could tend to try to obstruct the holding of a National Committee plenum whereas, don't forget, the PC is subordinate to the NC. So this provision was put into the resolution to make crystal clear that, while nobody can be allowed to obstruct the PC in executing the duties assigned to it by the NC and by the party constitution, the PC at all times remains subordinate to the NC. If, at any time, from anywhere within the NC, there is a desire expressed for a plenum to take up some matter the PC is handling, and if a majority of the NC wants that plenum, it must be held, whether the PC likes it or not. Now, we haven't had occasion to use that provision, but it's a very good provision to have in the basic document.

Those were the essentials of the additions in the 1953 resolution. The next changes resulted from new party experiences subsequent to the Cochranite episode. These led to a recodification of the party's organizational principles in 1965, brought about by organizational reflexes to new political differences that developed inside the party. At the outset, these differences centered on the Chinese question, the Black struggle, the Cuban Revolution, and reunification of the world movement. Diverse minority groups arose, each focusing on one or another of these issues. They were led variously by Swabeck, Kirk and Kaye, Robertson, Wohlforth, and sundry others ranging in political stature from I'd say gnat size to nit size.

What was politically common to this diversity of minorities was that each put forward its own quack political remedy to overcome the long isolation from the mass movement that the party had experienced because of adverse objective conditions during the period where cold war, witch hunt and McCarthyism predominated. Each of these groupings decided that the trouble wasn't in the objective situation, but that there was something wrong inside the party. What it was, of course, was the leadership. And they came up with new proposals, and put themselves forward as candidates to emulate Moses in leading the children of the party out of the wilderness.

Well the party rejected their views. And this threw them into calamity howling. They predicted political disaster for the party, and all of them ganged up in a fight against majority rule. This time it came in the form of demands that minorities be allowed to set their own norms of conduct inside the party. Matters began coming to a head after the 1963 party convention. At that convention, all the political issues had come before the party and had been argued back and forth, with generous time allowances for minorities to make reports and summaries on each of their positions, and the party definitively rejected the quack political remedies put forward by each of these minorities. That's what had happened politically.

Just on the eve of the convention, the party leadership learned that the Robertsonite faction was distributing a secret set of documents inside the party. After the convention the PC directed the National Control Commission to investigate this report of the secret Robertsonite documents.

The National Control Commission is a body set up under the provisions of the party constitution by the party convention. It is a body of five. As the constitution stipulates, four members of the Control Commission are elected by the convention itself to serve until the next convention, and the fifth is an NC member appointed by the NC to serve in whatever particular case may be before the Control Commission at a given moment. The Control Commission has the dual functions, 1.) overlooking, safeguarding and seeing to the rights of the party membership, and 2.) overlooking, safeguarding and seeing to the good and welfare of the party as a whole.

The Control Commission was given the assignment by the PC of investigating these documents. It obtained them and they were found to constitute a declaration of war on the party. They were really something, or, as you say nowadays, something else. They set forth a perspective of first recruiting people into their faction, where they would be indoctrinated with the Robertsonite program, and then, after sufficient boot camp training, getting them to join the party. But from the outset, they would be standing in opposition to the program of the party that they had just joined. That was one key prescription in these documents.

Another winged generalization in the Robertsonite documents was most descriptive of all. They inveighed against anybody getting any mistaken concepts of loyalty to a diseased shell, the diseased shell being the Socialist Workers Party.

Well, these documents were reported on to the PC, and the PC suspended the Robertsonite leaders from the party for disloyalty. And it also recommended that they be expelled by the NC. That was done at a plenum of the NC held in December, 1963. In the plenum debate on this question, Myra Weiss made a minority report in which she opposed the disciplinary action against the Robertsonites. She was given equal time with the majority reporter, which happened to be myself, and the whole matter was debated before the plenum.

All the minority leaders joined in this attack on majority rule that came in the form of opposition to the suspension of the Robertsonites for their disloyal conduct inside the party. Now this made it very plain that the Robertsonite caper was only one aggravated form of a serious internal party conflict on the organization question, and the situation as a whole posed the basic question as to the kind of a party we would have. Would it remain a Leninist-type, combat formation, or would it degenerate into an all-inclusive political hodge-podge?

The position put forward by the minority meant that they were demanding special license that would assure them an opportunity to do what they pleased under any circumstance. If the party as a whole was to be stripped of the right to regulate its internal affairs, as the minority demanded, the whole democratic centralist structure of the party would be undermined. The democratic principle of majority rule would be made a mockery. Discipline in public activity would be impossible. And internally, the party would have degenerated into a jungle characterized by perpetual factional warfare. Now this was the issue that was posed point-blank to the party by this outburst of opposition from the diverse minorities to the action of the PC and the NC in disciplining the Robertsonite leaders for their disloyalty. In tomorrow's concluding session I want to go in some detail into how this question was debated, how it was handled in the 1965 resolution, and some other important matters in the 1965 resolution, bringing things up to date with the present situation.

LECTURE 3

In yesterday's session, we arrived at the point in 1963 where the leaders of the Robertsonite faction were expelled for secretly circulating anti-party documents. All of the diverse organized minorities of that time ganged up in opposition to the disciplinary action which was taken against the Robertsonites because of their disloyalty. These minorities accused the party leadership of trying to introduce Stalinist monolithism into the party. This took the form, they said, of settling political differences by suppressing organized dissent. It was alleged that discipline applies only to the public activities of party members, and that official party bodies have no right to regulate a minority's internal party activities. Loyalty to the party, they contended, is only an idea. It can't be legislated. And disciplinary action, they alleged, can be taken only on specific proof of overt acts.

In rebuttal of the minority argument, the majority pointed out that loyalty to the party is not at all an abstract idea. It is a standard of political conduct. Without loyalty, a voluntary organization like the party would be absolutely unable to maintain discipline. Only comrades who believe in the party and are loyal to it will accept discipline. No one can be compelled to be loyal to the party, but they can be thrown out of its ranks if they are not. The very first codification of the party's organizational principles in 1938 stipulated that there must be unconditional loyalty to the party. At the same time, official party bodies were empowered to take disciplinary action against violators on this count.

With or without specific proof of overt acts, the party has the right in its own self-defense to expel self-indicted factional raiders who are out to wreck the organization. What were we supposed to do, we asked, stand here and wait for proof of a specific overt act, until these jokers have honeycombed the party to the point that it would be merely a hollow shell of itself, as they allege it to be? Not at all. The majority pointed out that the charge of retrogression towards Stalinist monolithism was designed to cloud the issue. It was a fake and it was a fraud. The real question was the right of the party as a whole to deal with internal disruption. As a voluntary organization, one which people are free to join or not according to their own inclinations, the party sets limits on the right of advocacy within its ranks. You cannot be a member of the SWP and advocate support to imperialist war, nor can you advocate crossing class lines into capitalist politics, nor can you espouse racism, nor can you propagate strikebreaking, just to mention a few examples.

And, similarly, the party proscribes advocacy of wrecking expeditions inside its ranks. In general, a disciplined party must regulate the conduct of organized groups in its ranks, just as it regulated the conduct of individual members.

In the aftermath of this debate, the disciplinary actions taken against the disloyal Robertsonite minority by the National Committee were ratified by the 1965 party convention. The other minorities, however, persisted in their course as if nothing whatever had been decided. And by 1967, all of them were out of the party. This came about in one of three general ways: either through expulsion for indiscipline and disloyalty, or from splits carried out on the initiative of one or another minority itself, or by disintegration of a minority through individual dropouts from the party.

The evolution of these particular minorities that we have been discussing presents a graphic illustration of the consequences of blind factionalism. Blind factionalists start by working on individuals privately, instilling one-sided political views that warp their capacity for objective political judgment. They become prejudiced in their opinions before they have had a chance to hear an open party debate of the disputed issues. This gives rise to the development of a tightly-knit faction that tends to become a party within the party. It has an inner logic in its development that impels it towards shaping its own program and establishing its own discipline, as against the program and discipline of the party. As a result, factionalism means war inside the party, and it always entails the danger of a split.

A relatively homogeneous party, where there is essential agreement on all sides as to the basic aspects of the party's program and principles, can resolve episodic differences without resorting to factionalism. This applies even where there are serious political disagreements over a given question. To justify the formation of a faction, the differences should be considered so fundamental that a showdown fight is necessary for control of the party. Ordinarily, a minority should do no more than form an ideological tendency. In this way, the adherents of a minority position have the mechanism through which to argue collectively for a change in the given policy under dispute. Their views should be presented openly before the whole party in a responsible and a disciplined way. While temporary groupings may arise in the party as a result of conjunctural political differences, such groupings should not be artificially perpetuated after the given question in dispute has been decided.

An artificially perpetuated grouping risks degenerating into an unprincipled clique. Such a grouping develops a tendency to act as a mutual advancement society inside the party: you rub my back, I'll rub yours; you push to enhance my prestige and position in the party, and I will reciprocate for you. This leads in turn to the substitution of relationships based on personal friendship for relationships based on political comradeship—and there is a very important difference between the two. Comradeship implies political collaboration despite personal relations. The important thing is not whether you like this or that individual member of the party. The important thing is whether you both agree on the program, the aims, the perspectives, the principles of the party. That is the only way you can hold a party together, even if it is politically homogeneous. Personal relations, however, are often transient. Friendship is a relationship that by its very nature is limited because it must be based on personal compatibility. You can't build a party on the basis of friendship. When a formation begins to degenerate into a clique, substituting friendship for comradeship, then it begins to put clique interests before those of the party. Its members more and more lose their sense of political objectivity in every respect. This leads to a gradual alienation of the clique members from the party, and the resultant loss of political bearings causes them to drift away from the party in time. That, by and large, has been the ultimate result of the development of clique formations in the history of the organization. They are a thing to be avoided like the plague. There's nothing principled and nothing justifiable about a clique from any point of view.

In 1965, the party adopted a new organizational resolution. That resolution affirmed and recodified the basic line of the 1938, 1940, and 1953 resolutions that we have previously discussed. New provisions were added rejecting the minority demand for dual disciplinary standards inside the party. A dissenting minority has the right to organize itself, the resolution states—this has always been the policy of our party. But its conduct is subject to regulation by official party bodies. These bodies must determine correct procedure both in public activity and in internal party affairs on the basis of the party's principles and its statutes. And in such matters, the resolution emphasized, the Political Committee may act on behalf of the National Committee in discharging these responsibilities of leadership, doing so under the control of the National Committee.

Taking cognizance of the present day objective conditions, and the specific stage of party development in 1965, the document also made some changes from the organizational provisions of an earlier time. Circumstances of the split in 1940 and the country's imminent entry into World War II had given rise to the specific provisions in the 1940 resolution on proletarianization. Taking note of the changed specific circumstances, the 1965 resolution modified the exclusive focus in the 1940 resolution on penetrating the workers movement, while retaining the perspective set forth in the 1940 resolution of building a proletarian revolutionary party.

Our basic political orientation in 1940 stemmed from the perspective that it was entirely possible for proletarian revolution in advanced capitalist countries to erupt out of World War II, just as the Bolshevik Revolution had erupted out of World War I. History was to show, however, that the processes of world revolution were to take a different course. The objective premises were present for proletarian revolution in advanced countries, but due to the crisis of leadership in the working class, the possibilities were aborted and the course of world revolution did not take that immediate road. Instead, the revolutionary process showed its next emphasis in the area of the colonial and semi-colonial countries. The unfolding objective process from 1945 on brought about the specific set of objective conditions that are fundamental to the radicalization that is developing and gaining momentum in our country today.

Now, everything that is most essential to the changed objective conditions, as we perceive it today, was already, at least in its broad lines, perceptible in 1965. So modifications were made in the 1965 resolution. Conjunctural passages setting forth specific steps toward proletarianization of the party, as they had been delineated in 1940, were omitted from the 1965 recodification of our organizational principles. These passages had been applicable in those earlier circumstances, but a modified approach was obviously required in today's objective conditions. Instead of the one-sided emphasis on penetration of the organized labor movement and on reaching the proletariat in the working class neighborhoods, the 1965 recodification calls for efforts to penetrate all sectors of the mass movement: labor organizations within industry; the unemployed; the movements of oppressed nationalities—Blacks, Chicanos, Puerto Ricans and others—that are becoming radicalized and in which workers, by the way, predominate; college campuses and high schools, where the students are showing more and more of a tendency to turn toward socialist ideas. These were the essential sectors of the mass movement listed in the resolution. But the general concept on which this list was based automatically implies attention to new developments that could not be specifically anticipated in 1965, for example, the women's liberation movement that is unfolding today. The overall aim of the modified codification of this perspective in the resolution was to reach out to all opponents of the capitalist status quo and seek to bring the militants into our revolutionary party.

Note is also taken in the recodified resolution of 1965 concerning the assimilation of non-workers into the party. It is stressed that non-workers must consciously break from alien class influence. Your role in the revolutionary movement is not a question of what your class origins are, but of what you do after you get here. Do you come in 100%?—in the last analysis it's got to be that. It's got to be 100% if you're really going to be a revolutionist and identify with the class through its vanguard revolutionary party. This is a very important thing to keep carefully in mind.

Our long term perspective remains the same. The working class is as yet lagging in the process of radicalization, but before there can be a revolution, the working class must come into the action massively, with all its basic historic power. If you stop and think for a minute, there is a little touch of historic irony. At the very moment when the organized labor movement, as such, is the most laggard in the process of radicalization, the vanguard revolutionary party, that based itself on the perspective of a revolution powered by the working class and led by a revolutionary proletarian party, is gaining more and more rapid headway in extending its influence inside the presently developing radicalization.

It is through the instrumentality of the party, that the non-worker today identifies with the working class in the deepest and most complete sense. All that is required is that you be a 100 per center. You don't have to be a genius. Not everybody can be a genius. I've seen some that thought they were, though they weren't quite as smart as some other geniuses that I have seen. All you have to be is for real. That's all. Just be for real. Do the best you can, be 100% and identify with the working class through its vanguard revolutionary party, and you're on the right track in the whole new historic process of radicalization, and moving toward potential revolution.

Concerning the infusion of new blood into the leadership of the party, the 1940 resolution put primary stress on young workers who show ability through their activity in the unions. The 1965 document broadens the field of candidates for the National Committee to include young party activists who show ability through their activity in one or another sector of the mass movement. There were two reasons for this modification. One relates to the widened areas of potential penetration into the mass movement, under the distinct forms in which the developing radicalization is unfolding today. Another relates to the special problem of transition in party leadership. That is another matter that the party has been giving very conscious attention to ever since the first recruits out of the developing youth radicalization began to come toward our movement back in the beginning of the 1960's.

To give you an example of the tempo of this development I might say in passing that there are several comrades in leading national positions in the party today who were first attracted to the party in the 1960 presidential campaign and who attended their first party convention in 1961. Here it is nine years later, and you'll observe that we've come quite a distance in carrying out this transition in leadership. We are doing it with the greatest consciousness. It is not simply a matter of recognizing that the older comrades aren't going to live forever. That isn't the only thing. Revolutions are made by the young. Not only must the revolutionary masses have a vanguard party that knows what it's doing and is able to lead them to victory, but the party must also be staffed by young people who have both the dynamism of youth and the forced draft education in all aspects of the problems of revolution, that they get through a vanguard party such as ours. We have sought consciously to make these transitions as rapidly as we could, doing it in such a way that younger comrades are more and more able to take responsibility for central leadership roles in the party. We are also doing it in such a way that older comrades, who haven't got the juice and life expectancy they once had, are able to be present more and more as advisors to help the younger comrades learn by doing.

There are two aspects of the transition towards a younger leadership that are very basic. One is that the older of the central leaders are not arbitrarily choosing who among the younger comrades should be advanced to more responsible leadership positions in the party. On the contrary, they are watching very carefully to see how the younger comrades develop in their work in the party, to facilitate giving them as many opportunities as is possible to prove themselves as leaders in the eyes of the ranks of the party. Second, the question of who will become the young leaders is determined finally by the opinion that the party ranks arrive at concerning a given individual's capacity to lead and his or her trustworthiness as a leader.

I should add, also, that the 1965 resolution dropped the 1940 provision that student youth must serve an apprenticeship in the workers movement before being a candidate for the National Committee. As I told you yesterday, that proviso stemmed from the specific negative experiences we had with a petty bourgeois opposition in the party at that time. But this is not applicable under today's conditions. So that proviso was just simply dropped from the basic organizational document, and it is not applied.

Another change in the 1965 resolution related to the references to the Fourth International in the 1940 document. The April 1940 resolution listed the programmatic documents on which SWP doctrine is officially based, including specific reference to the documents of the Fourth International, of which the SWP had been one of the founding sections. Later in 1940, the Voorhis law was passed, which made it impossible for the party to be organizationally affiliated with an international movement. So, in December 1940, at a special party convention after the passage of the Voorhis law, the SWP disaffiliated from the Fourth International and assumed the role of being a sympathizer of the world Trotskyist movement. In the light of the antidemocratic legislation in this country, that was the only relationship we could have. Now, in view of that changed situation, the 1965 recodification of our organizational principles again modified those earlier references to the Fourth International. Instead of the previous general reference to the documents of the Fourth International, it specifically listed the Transitional Program of 1938, which was adopted at the founding congress of the Fourth International, the American Theses of 1946, which were adopted at a convention of the SWP at that time, and other programmatic documents of the Trotskyist movement.

This now takes us back to the initial point of departure in our discussion, namely, the fundamental relationship between organization and politics. Our goal is to align the United States with the world march toward socialism. From that flows our fraternal interest in the development of the world Trotskyist movement. International exchanges of political thought help us to project policies within the United States in the light of world trends. We are better able to work in consonance with a world revolutionary strategy.

In our political work, we proceed through the essential conceptions of the system of transitional demands adopted by the founding convention of the Fourth International. These stem from today's conditions and the levels of political consciousness in the broad mass. They are aimed to meet urgent social needs of the time, and are pointed in an anticapitalist direction. The transitional demands as a whole meld into a program leading toward one final conclusion—the conquest of power by the working class and its allies. All our mass work has clearly defined immediate political aims. We seek everywhere in the mass movement to build left wing formations founded on a class struggle program, and through these formations, we orient toward a fight for mass leadership on the basis of the program. We can expect our efforts to be facilitated by the developing processes of mass radicalization. Class issues will come into increasingly sharp focus in contemporary society. The need for opposition to capitalist rule will become plainer and plainer to the masses. Consequently the fight over program will grow increasingly acute, and the crisis of mass leadership will become more intense. As the American Theses of 1946 predict, this process will in time open the road to a revolutionary solution of the social crisis. The showdown battles for the communist future of mankind will be fought right here in this country, and we confidently predict that the working class will show its capacity to fulfill its historic role in that showdown.

All this will be possible provided there is a combat party capable of giving revolutionary leadership. To fulfill that role, the party must be politically cohesive and organizationally disciplined. Its structure and its practices must be rooted in the concepts of democratic centralism. From the very beginning the Trotskyist movement in this country has based itself on these Leninist concepts. The party has fought off every attack on its organizational principles and has preserved its organizational character. And the task now is to take it from there, particularly through younger hands, into the next phases of party-building work.

Toward that end, I will conclude with a recapitulation of some key features of democratic centralism as they derive from Lenin's theory and practice, and as they have been made more concrete through the experiences of the SWP.

Members join the party voluntarily. Therefore, the party has the right to define the conditions for membership in its ranks. It does so in terms of its program and its organizational principles which serve the program. As a combat formation, the party must have several basic attributes. These include firmness of political line, unity in action, and discipline in all internal party affairs, with all members unconditionally loyal to the party. Such qualities make it possible to go up against the ruling class as one party, with one program. Democratic centralist norms require a free and democratic internal party atmosphere. Room must be provided for the expression of dissident views. The right to organize tendencies and factions must be protected. All individuals and all tendencies must be enabled to contribute to the development of the party, and to the shaping of its leading cadres. Minorities are entitled to present their views in internal party discussion, at the proper time and in an appropriate manner, as determined by the party. Once a decision has been made on disputed issues by majority vote, the minority must subordinate itself in action to the majority. The minority may retain its views, but it must help carry out the majority decision.

Between conventions, authority becomes centralized. The party confronts the outside world with a single policy: that of the majority. Both external and internal activities are regulated by the official party bodies. Indiscipline and disloyalty are treated as crimes that bring punishment—if you don't do that, you'll never in a thousand years build a combat party. In this way, the party maintains its role as a revolutionary vanguard. Its character as a combat organization is safeguarded, unity in action is preserved, firmness of political line is assured, and the party is able to maintain its principles.

Only along this general line of organizational structure and principles can the party fulfill its historical tasks in the revolutionary struggle for socialism.

EXCERPTS FROM THE QUESTION AND ANSWER PERIODS

LECTURE 1

QUESTION: The party is small now. When it becomes larger, is there a way to select or nominate a National Committee, other than through a nominating commission? From what I have heard it is really difficult for the nominating commission to go over all the different people who are proposed.

ANSWER: Let's abstract from the question of size, and look at it from the point of view of the basic concepts. The basic concept is to provide maximum safeguards, to see that the membership of the organization makes the decisions about who are going to be the leaders, and that a leadership, once in office, cannot by virtue of its own position in office artificially perpetuate itself, and become what Trotsky once referred to as irremovable senators. That is the basic idea. In this regard, there is a very useful work written by Comrade Cannon. It is available in an internal information bulletin that was published in advance of the last convention (April 1969) under the title, "Problems of Leadership Selection and Leadership Structure." It is also available in Comrade Cannon's *Letters From Prison* (Pathfinder Press, 1968, 1973), pp. 280–85, 290–96 [2021 printing]. It was a letter that Comrade Cannon wrote when he and many other party leaders were in prison in 1944 and the party was for the first time in a complete sense beginning to develop the nominating commission method with respect to the party convention of that year. It is well worth your while to study the whole bulletin because it takes up, step by step, several key phases in the period from 1944 up to the latter part of the 1960's in which we were grappling with various aspects of the problem of leadership selection and structure.

You will find in that article by Comrade Cannon a review of diverse methods that were used to elect a leadership in radical organizations. He mentions, among other things, how the social democratic fakers used to operate behind the scenes in the Socialist Party. He describes an earlier stage in our movement, which represented an advance from that method, in which the leadership came in openly with a slate. It was then up to the membership to decide whether or not to ratify the slate. We were uneasy with that procedure, because, while it was subject to membership ratification, the very fact that the slate was compiled by the leadership put a certain pressure on the ranks. Comrade Cannon describes how we passed from that to the process of the nominating commission.

The nominating commission method had as a corollary another very careful policy on the part of the leadership.

You will find a discussion of this in the same bulletin. I gave a report to a plenum of the National Committee of the SWP in 1962 in which we were raising for consideration the category of advisory membership on the National Committee, and I took some care to describe the attitude of the central leaders of the party towards the work of the nominating commission. The central leaders did not mess in it. I pointed out that at the prior convention the leadership of the party had, for the first time since the development of the nominating commission back in 1944, gone before the nominating commission with some recommendations. The reason was that we were grappling with a problem of transition in leadership, and the nominating commission just didn't know how to proceed—we had to find some way of breaking a logjam that had developed in the National Committee itself. So the leadership went to the nominating commission, explained the problem to them, and said, "All we can recommend is that you do the best you can at this time, and before the next convention, we'll try to have this logjam broken and you can operate in a better way." And that is the way it worked out. We developed the category of advisory membership, and that broke the logjam in the National Committee and opened the way to bringing some younger comrades in to the National Committee. It is worth your while to read that article too. I cite these articles again, from a basic point of view, that the ranks make the decision about leadership. While leaders must lead in everything, including the question of leadership, there is a big difference between trying, in an objective way, to give assistance to the ranks in resolving a leadership problem, and throwing weight around inhibiting the ranks from exercising their judgment, or obstructing the exercise of judgment in the ranks.

Now as to the size of the party affecting the selection of the leadership. As an organization grows, as the magnitude of its activities, the scope of its functions, the forms of organization develop, it seems to me that you will find repeated, at the regional levels, in a microcosm at first, a sort of reproduction of the general problem of picking a national leadership. Instead of a national leadership evolving directly out of branch leaderships or from comrades who are given specialized tasks which they discharge well in one or another department of the party's activity, there will be a certain preliminary testing of the leadership capacity of comrades on the basis of how they evolve in their leadership role on a regional basis. The forms will change, but the essence will remain the same. Now, I would not hazard any kind of a priori formula about the exact manner in which leadership selection would be carried through as an organization grows. I will just stress these points: 1.) Whatever the specific form of operation, the ranks must decide the question of leadership. The leadership must not push the ranks around, maneuver with them, and perpetuate itself against the will of the ranks; 2.) I am confident that as the comrades study this question in more and more detail, it will be solved.

QUESTION: How does democratic centralism apply to the international Trotskyist movement?

ANSWER: During the conflict with the Cochran faction that involved also a split in the International that took place in 1953, Comrade Cannon made a speech on this question to a meeting of the majority caucus in the party at that time, in which you will find some very rich material to give you food for thought. The speech is found in the educational bulletin entitled "Defending the Revolutionary Party and Its Perspectives."* Comrade Cannon pointed out that there is a pronounced difference between the application of democratic centralism within a national party and within the International. It is not a question of whether or not there is validity to democratic centralism with respect to an International. It is a question of how far the International has progressed in its development.

The International, as such, is not as wholly definable as a completely crystallized organization, as is a party in a given country. As Comrade Cannon pointed out, if international leaders are too hasty in throwing their weight around with regard to the work in national sections, this can have the effect of obstructing the development of a leadership within a national section, rather than helping along the process. In the last analysis an International has to be based before everything else on the presence of strong national sections in the various countries. Strong national sections have to evolve on the basis of their own living experiences in seeking to put the basic Trotskyist program into practice in their particular country. In the course of that process, they develop basic cadres, they begin to develop and train a leadership. And an equilibrium evolves between membership and leadership that gives an internal stability to the organization. That can't be accomplished from anywhere except in that country.

Moreover, in respect to international relations there's a difference between problems in one or another country, and problems in one or another branch within a country. Between party branches there can be nuances, or even significant differences with regard to how to apply a given policy in a given locality, but branch policy still falls within the framework of the same national framework. Branches are an integral part of a cohesive national political operation. But different countries are at different stages of development. There are three

---

* The May 18, 1953, speech, "Internationalism and the SWP," is now printed in James P. Cannon, *Speeches to the Party* (Pathfinder, 1973).

broad categories of countries in the world: some are advanced capitalist countries, some are now workers states, and some are colonial countries. Even within these basic areas, there are different conditions within each country. Therefore, there has to be a certain degree of fundamental party building that must take place within those countries on the basis of what can be developed within the country itself. In that process an international leadership can only help. So from this point of view, the relation of an international leadership to national sections of the International is altogether different from the relation of a national leadership to the branches of an organization within a country.

QUESTION: Would you go into the problems of leadership selection during a period of extreme reaction, for example if the party were to go underground, and it was impossible to convene the party ranks on a national scale to oversee the selection of leadership.

ANSWER: That's what you call a loaded question. But I am going to yield a little to the temptation to answer it. First of all, just let me make this point in passing. While under certain circumstances it may be necessary for a revolutionary party to go underground, don't ever do it voluntarily. That is another one of the stupidities of these New Left geniuses. If a party is driven underground, if it has no alternative, it does not change its basic concepts. It just does the best it can in the light of the given situation. And even if a movement is underground, there can be various degrees of being underground. Sometimes, it might not mean much more than the fact that you cannot easily operate publicly without getting picked off by the political police. In a more severe case, it might necessitate extreme care in functioning even in an underground way, because of the dangers. But whatever the circumstance, the party tries to apply its basic concepts as best it can. If the party is forced underground—Lenin set the example as well as anybody ever did—well, you try to have an underground convention. You try to maintain all the basic forms of operation.

Let me add a second point. The combat situation that is involved in a revolutionary struggle against capitalism is one that always involves diverse dangers in one or another form, at one or another stage. This simply emphasizes how very important the leadership question is. It underlines how vital it is that a party has leaders who have been schooled and tested in the life of the party, who genuinely have the support of the party ranks, who know what they are doing, who are dedicated to the party.

Sometimes it seems a little abstract to talk about what a leader's basic attitude should be toward the party. It is not abstract at all, because there is an awful lot riding on it. It is said that there is a certain honor that goes with leadership, but let me tell you this, that when you take on any kind of leadership role in a revolutionary party, then you have taken on a responsibility that adds considerable dimension to what is rightfully expected of you. A leader cannot wear two coats. You cannot wear one coat as a leader, then put on another and become a private citizen and do whatever you damn please! Anybody who does that is not yet a mature leader. And, in every respect, the vicissitudes of combat in a revolutionary struggle are such that at all junctures the most careful attention must be given to the problem of leadership selection. And, in that, no one is to be trusted more than the rank and file of an educated revolutionary organization. So long as you proceed on the basis that to be a leader in the party you have to get the votes, that means that that vote is going to be for real, and the party is going to come out pretty good on the question of leaders. If a mistake is made here and there in selection, it can always be corrected. In the history of the party there has been more than one occasion in which a comrade has been elected to the Committee and dropped later.

It is a matter of the most extreme importance that the party have, at all times, leaders who have earned the confidence of the rank and file, leaders in whom the rank and file can justly place their trust. If you have that, then you can ride out a rough period. We had an example in the early 1940s when a considerable section of the top leadership of the party was convicted under the Smith Act. When the Supreme Court refused to hear our appeal in the fall of 1943, we all had to go to the pokey. This took a big slice right off the top of the leadership, and tested the party's ability to make up for the temporary losses. But comrades who were part of the broad leadership team, including a number of comrades who had previously played a secondary role in the leadership, came forward, stepped in, filled the gap when several of the top leaders went to prison, and the party went right ahead.

This points out another aspect about the leadership question. The idea of a leadership by stars is not worth a damn. A star is all right in Hollywood. But be mighty careful about them from the point of view of a revolutionary movement. Talented people, yes! Grandstanders, no! You need a team. And a team in the most complete sense, is a composite of comrades playing one and another leading role, at one and another level in the general leadership structure of the party, with one or another degree of experience, but all of whom try to act together in the best interest of the party, and who at all times are trying to help younger promising comrades develop as leaders. So there is a central primary leadership, a developing body of secondary leaders, and promising candidates for secondary leaders developing in the ranks. In that way problems such as we experienced in 1943–1944 do not create a crisis at all.

There is another example, taken from the 1934 Teamsters' strike in Minneapolis, showing how this works in a larger organization. One day the military raided the strike headquarters and picked up several of the top leaders. The governor had a little scheme cooked up. They grabbed off several of the top leaders and threw them in the military stockade. Then the governor sent some of his stooges out to contact some of the strikers. These minor labor fakers from the AFL contacted some of the strikers, saying the governor wanted to meet a rank and file committee. Well he got a rank and file committee! Kelly Postal, Ray Rainbolt, and Jack Maloney. Now, the governor liked to make like he was a working stiff; he pulled out a pack of Yankee Girl chewing tobacco and handed it to them— when he got it back there was no more tobacco. Then, he said, "I want to negotiate with you." They said, "Fine governor, we'll negotiate, there are just some things we want first: 1.) Let our leaders out of jail. 2.) Give us back our headquarters, and 3.) take your goddamned troops off the street. Then we'll negotiate." That's as far as the governor ever got.

This was the secondary strike leadership. But it was a secondary strike leadership that had been developed with the same consciousness that we build leadership formations in the revolutionary party. The central leaders of that strike were conscious Trotskyist revolutionists, men like Ray Dunne and Carl Skogland who played a key role in building the party itself. Here was an example in a mass struggle of how decisive the leadership question is. The whole strike could have been lost at a stroke if there had not been a strong secondary leadership. Just think of how many times the capitalists have won battles because the leadership was limited to a bunch of stars. It did not matter how intelligent they were, they were fatheaded in this sense—they imagined they were entitled to some kind of corner on the leadership, and did not want to help others develop as leaders for fear of developing rivals. The capitalist class can then step in and lop this leadership off in a fight, leave the movement leaderless, and it can go right down the drain.

LECTURE 2

QUESTION: What was the social composition of the Cochran faction?

ANSWER: In the case of the Cochran faction, you had a situation in which a key component was made up of trade unionists. When you think of this eventuality, one is reminded of Trotsky's preoccupation with the question of relations between trade unionists and the party. Time and again he pointed out that the very nature of a trade union, an organization that fights for immediate demands in terms of the contemporary situation, has within itself the fundamental prerequisites for generating reformist attitudes. A revolutionist in the unions could get a little disoriented were it not for the relationship of the party to the individual member. Let me call your attention to the document, "Communism and Syndicalism," contained in the pamphlet *Trotsky on the Trade Unions*, published by Pathfinder Press. "Trade Unions in the Epoch of Imperialist Decay," is another document by Trotsky.* Also look up the trade union resolution adopted by the party at the 1954 convention, "Class Struggle Policy in the Unions" (*SWP Internal Bulletin*, Vol. XVI, No. 2).

This resolution was adopted in 1954, the year

---

* The articles by Trotsky are available in *Trade Unions in the Epoch of Imperialist Decay*, (Pathfinder Press, 1990).

following the Cochranite split, which came to its culmination in November, 1953. It came just as the objective turn was beginning with respect to McCarthyism. The army-McCarthy hearings were unfolding, and there were a few signs of gestation toward action in the unions. This resolution really sought to recapitulate the trade union situation across the whole 14-year period from the adoption of a basic resolution on the trade union question at the 1940 convention. It tried to examine several aspects of the dynamic of the relationship between the party and the party man or woman in the trade unions. The latter part of that resolution calls attention to the fact that at the given juncture, there were a number of things that the trade union comrades might want to say in the unions, but weren't in a position to say them right then and there without risking victimization for no good reason. Therefore the party would speak for them, through articles by party members in the the *Militant*.

If you read that resolution, you'll find that it's put expressly in terms of the party talking to and for its trade union members at that juncture. It also delineates the overwhelming importance of the general relationship between the party and the party member in the union. The party is the means of helping the party member in the mass movement, where reformist impulses are generating, to be a revolutionist.

Now in the case of the Cochranite faction, what happened was that they lost faith in the party. In the Cochran faction there was an unprincipled combination. One section of this faction, manifested by Clarke, held the line espoused by Pablo in the International, the theory of the self-reform of the Soviet bureaucracy, and its bureaucratic counterparts in the workers' states in Eastern Europe. The trade union wing, manifested particularly by Cochran, was developing a line of adaptation to the expectation of self-reform of the American trade union bureaucracy. Each assumed the self-reform of bureaucracy, and each had lost faith in the possibility of building a revolutionary combat party, as ours is, that would in due course be able to challenge these bureaucrats. This is what they had in common, and they made an unprincipled bloc, although they were looking in two different directions. One gang was becoming a little soft on Stalinism. The other was becoming soft on the trade union bureaucrats.

When you have a minority that is coming in with a line that is calculated to change some important aspect of the party program, you'll often find that they try to smuggle it in, they talk around the question and toe-dance around the question, and never say explicitly what they mean. But if you watch and you listen, you'll find somebody in the ranks of that kind of a movement who will sooner or later blurt out in an unvarnished way the exact direction in which they're going. And this happened in the Cochran fight. At one key juncture in a debate between the majority and the minority in the Cochran fight, one of the Cochranites blurted out that Reuther was to the left of the workers. He put in one sentence the distilled essence of what had happened to the mentality of this trade union wing of the Cochran faction.

This example helps to show that disaffection can come from a section of workers in the movement as well as from a petty bourgeois section within the movement. In each case, what is basic is the pressure of alien class influences in the environment that they are in, and the loss of their sea anchor of continued belief in the program of the party, faith in the future of the party, and a loyal attitude toward the party.

QUESTION: Could you say some more about the role played by Pablo in the 1952 internal struggle within our party?

ANSWER: Well, that's a subject in itself, and we really can't get into it in any real detail without getting clear afield from the subject before us. I would simply point out that out of this struggle, something else arose on the organization side. While it is not yet codified in the basic doctrine of the movement, in the sense that we've sought to codify some of our principles in our organizational resolutions, something very clear was brought out about the relationship between an international movement and the sections and about relations within the leadership of an international movement.

The essence of Pablo's policy was an expectation that World War III was going to break out momentarily. And the moment the war broke out, revolution was going to explode, and this war-revolution crisis would compel the bureaucracies in the workers' states to self-reform and adjust on a life and death basis to this changed situation. Therefore it was important for the Trotskyist movement to get into these organizations forthwith and be there to give leadership, step to the fore, and take the control when the process began to happen. That was his essential line. We disagreed with it, and I think history showed we were right.

On the organization side, Pablo's impatience to put over his line caused him to engage in some organizational measures that are absolutely incompatible with democratic centralism. First I should explain the structure of the International: there are the sections of the International. The world congress of the International is the equivalent of a convention of the party; the congress elects an International Executive Committee, which is the equivalent of the National Committee of the party; the IEC elects a Secretariat, which is the equivalent of the Political Committee in the party; and then the Secretariat has a bureau which is more or less the counterpart of the Administrative Committee of the Political Committee in our party. On this basis Pablo started to lay down the following lines of procedure. Anybody in the bureau who disagreed with him was bound in the next body on the basis of majority rule. Suppose there are three on the bureau and one of them agrees with Pablo and the other disagrees. According to Pablo, the one that disagrees has got to obey majority rule of the bureau in the next body, the Secretariat. Then, if he gets a majority in the Secretariat on this basis, they've got to go, as a bloc, to the IEC, and then theoretically the IEC has to go to the whole movement as a bloc. Well that's a vulgarization of democratic centralism.

There was another practice of Pablo's that was in violation of democratic centralism, in its essence, and obstructive, devastatingly obstructive to the building of an International. We were talking yesterday about the importance of every section of the International evolving into an organization that has forged its own cadres, developed its own leadership, and is able to work in objective collaboration with an international movement. An international movement can't by appointment make leaders out of them. When a majority in a given party was against Pablo's line, he set out to maneuver behind the backs of the leadership and the majority of the party to create a faction against them. He gave the faction aid and comfort in the International. Now you can't build a world movement that way. That is not the way democratic centralism operates.

So in these respects on the international sphere, at least on the organization side, which is all I care to comment on at the moment, some very important lessons were learned in that experience about the problem of building a world movement, and about the problem of relationships between leadership and membership, which in this case takes the form of a relationship between leading international bodies and national sections of the movement.

QUESTION: What happened to the Shachtmanite structure after the 1940 split?

ANSWER: They started on the basis that they were going to continue democratic centralism. But it's worthwhile to look at it politically first.

The Burnham-Shachtman-Abern opposition was an unprincipled political combination. They subordinated important political differences within the combination to the desire for knitting themselves together in a common faction for purposes of overturning the program and regime of the party. That's the essence. In this instance the debate itself showed that Burnham had never come all the way to Trotskyism. Among other things he had never come to accept the dialectical method. There's a wonderful article by Trotsky that you'll find in *In Defense of Marxism*, where he takes this question up. Burnham was evolving very rapidly to the right, and he was already then anti-Soviet, period. Shachtman was straddling. He found it uncomfortable to defend the Soviet Union, to go out on the hustings in this country and say he defended the Soviet Union against imperialist attack, when Stalin had just signed a pact with Hitler.

Shachtman, however, was willing to make a small reservation: in the event of an actual invasion of the Soviet Union by imperialist forces, then he said he would be forced to defend it. Burnham, however, overrode that. Shachtman's primary concern was to get loose from the democratic centralist control of the party, so he knuckled under to Burnham. Abern, on the other hand, who was a leader of a clique, thought all the time that the whole thing was about the organization question. He didn't pay too much attention to the Russian question. This guy was a congenital cliquist, and saw a first class chance to get some licks in. That was his motivation. So they made their split.

Well they started out saying that they were going to show how things could be done. They evolved their third camp posture, and said they were going to continue the basic Leninist concepts of democratic centralism and so on. But they had scarcely gotten out of the party when Burnham walked away. He went all the way over to the right, and the next thing you know, he was writing a book called *The Managerial Revolution*. He wound up in McCarthy's stable back in the early 1950s. Shachtman played footsie with the possibility of getting some kind of support against us in the International, and tried a little unity caper toward us, around 1947. But it took no effort at all to show that the whole thing was a trick and a hoax, that he had not a serious thought toward the party.

Shachtman evolved in a social-democratic direction. He went on to join the Socialist Party and become one of the leading right wing social democrats. Shachtman had one small misfortune. He was born to be a lawyer, he really was. If he was working well, he had many talents. If he was working with somebody in whom he had confidence and respect as a leader, and would work under that leadership, he could do some very wonderful things. But put him out on his own, and he couldn't lead and organize the demand for ice water in hell! It was one of these cases where a person that could have been very valuable up to a given point got a little too big for his britches and wound up a nothing, politically. So they started with all the pretensions that they were going to go ahead and show us how to build a party in this country, and the whole thing collapsed. It collapsed primarily for the reason that the politics of the whole course they took was fundamentally defective.

LECTURE 3

QUESTION: Can you explain on an organization level how a loyal minority should conduct itself?

ANSWER: Let me give you an example from party history of what I always considered a thoroughly outstanding and serious minority in the party. It arose in a dispute in the latter part of the 1940s, over the nature of the states in Eastern Europe. With the exception of Yugoslavia, these states had been taken over essentially by a military bureaucratic process due to the presence of the Red Army. The question was posed: what is the nature of these states? A minority developed in the party that took the view that they were in essence workers' states. They said that these states couldn't be called "degenerated workers' states," in the sense that the Soviet Union became a degenerated workers' state after Stalinism developed. They arrived at the conclusion they could best be characterized terminologically as "deformed workers' states." That is, they didn't come into being like a healthy infant, as the Bolshevik revolution did, with all its limbs and natural faculties intact, and then degenerate later. They were born with a deformity, because of the presence of Stalinism in the situation. That was the essence of the position taken by the minority.

The party did not agree with this, at first. As a matter of fact, there was considerable reluctance in the party to really face the question. But this minority thought it was important.

The minority included comrades like Joe Hansen, Tom Kerry, and Bert Cochran. They organized an ideological tendency. They were experienced hands. They did not set up a faction. They knew that while it is sometimes necessary to set up a faction, a faction is a dangerous thing, in and of itself. A faction is a lethal weapon, which has its own logic. A given leadership can set up a faction to serve a particular aim, but, as Engels said in the introduction to *The Dialectics of Nature*, when you set controlled forces in motion according to a plan, you also set in motion uncontrolled forces with the result that there is often a wide disproportion between aims and results. The whole implication of setting up a faction is to attack the program and regime of the party. You organize a faction, and I'll make book that from the very first, you'll pick up everybody who's got a gripe or a grievance in the party. It's instinctively sensed that a faction is aimed against the existing regime and there may be a gripe or a grievance against the regime from one or another quarter.

A leader can organize a faction, only to find out in the end that the faction tends to take control of the leader. Shachtman learned that to his great surprise in the 1939–40 fight. At the outset in that fight,

Shachtman thought he was the big rainmaker. But lo and behold, he found himself a captive, and he was treated rather cynically. There's a story about a conference that the Shachtmanite faction held in Cleveland a few weeks before the split. They had finished their labors of the day at this hotel where they were staying, and they had all retired. Burnham, a cynical s.o.b. if I ever met one—he was just the kind of character who would do a thing like this—had one of his cronies run upstairs to tell Shachtman and Abern and the others that a message had just come from Trotsky. So they came dashing down into the lobby dressed in their robes, and he sat there and sneered at them: "You—independent thinkers!" Well, you can see Shachtman was no longer quite in control of his faction.

Now in the case of this difference in the latter 1940s, what the comrades did was to collaborate in discussing their views among themselves. Through a process of collective thinking, they arrived at a generally accepted concept among themselves as to what the party line should be about the definition of the nature of the buffer states in East Europe. Then, in a most responsible way, they awaited the first opportunity with the opening of an internal party discussion, to present their views in writing and at the appropriate moment, to argue for their views in discussion. And they were eventually able to convince a majority of the party that they were essentially right.

So you see, it's a very big mistake to think that you've got to organize for war in the party because you've got a difference of opinion. In the last analysis, you can't scare anybody in this kind of a party. If there were people in this party who would be scared because somebody threatened them, they wouldn't be here in the first place, because the capitalist class is threatening you all the time. You've got to reason with people. If you assume a hostile, combative attitude and try to slug your way through, you're more liable to make people angry than to convince them. But if you proceed in a reasoned way, then different criteria apply. Everybody gets a chance to hear what you have to say, and everybody gets a chance to hear what the rest of the party has to say, and they can think it out. If you proceed on the basis of reason, if you try in a responsible, loyal, and disciplined way, using the power of ideas and the force of argument to convince people, if you are right and the party is wrong, then the party will rectify itself.

It is also necessary to have a little patience. I'll spend a moment on this question first from the point of view of a leader. The duty of a leader is to try to be a little bit ahead of the ranks in grasping the feeling of what is happening in the objective process, and thinking out the most effective ways for the party to act in the given situation. It is also a duty of a leader to be patient. If a leader gets an idea for something that the party ought to do, that leader shouldn't rush out and start knocking heads if everybody doesn't jump right up and say, "Good! That's the best idea that's ever come down the pike! Let's get at it!" A leader has got to have enough patience, enough understanding, enough of the pedagogic sense to first explain the idea, give the comrades a chance to think about it, and give the organization time to bring its consciousness abreast of the situation that the given leader seeks to call to the party's attention.

Similarly, with any person who has a dissident view, whether a leader or simply a rank and filer. On the one hand, of course all party members have the right to present their views. On the other hand, it is necessary to have a little patience with the party. A time for discussion arises, and one with a dissident view presents his or her thoughts. The discussion ends and a vote is taken. Suppose the dissident view does not prevail. The loyal thing to do then is to say, "Well, it didn't work this time. But I still think it's important, and so at the next occasion for discussion, I will raise the matter again. In the meantime, I'll think about it, I'll watch what happens." Now something else operates here, in between discussion periods. Political life is always moving. Something can happen between one discussion and the next. The person with a dissident view as against the majority opinion in the party can find that either the evolution of political reality between one party discussion and the next can give new impetus to the dissident view, or it can convince the comrade with the dissident opinion that he or she was wrong. That's always possible too, you know.

The object of this procedure is always the good and welfare of the party. That, and nothing else! Always as a loyal member of the party, see yourself in relation to the party. Never look at the party in relation to yourself. The question is, what can I do—whatever are my abilities, talents, energies, and capacities—to contribute to the cause in which I believe, and to which the party is dedicated? Never ask, what can the party do to advance my personal career, or magnify my ego? Always see yourself in relation to the party, never the party in relation to yourself. Those are some of the guidelines that I would suggest as to how a loyal minority ought to conduct itself.

QUESTION: Would you comment on the concepts and problems of building a team leadership, especially in a period of expansion like we're going through right now?

ANSWER: First, let me refer you to some background material that's worth looking at on this question. One is a speech made by Comrade Cannon at the November 1953 plenum of the SWP where the Cochranites were expelled for disloyalty. It is entitled "Factional Struggle and Party Leadership" and it appears in the Education for Socialists bulletin *Defending the Revolutionary Party and its Perspectives*.* Another is a bulletin put out prior to the 1969 party convention under the title of "Problems of Leadership Selection and Leadership Structure." Both of these are well worth reading.

In Comrade Cannon's speech advancing the concept of a team leadership, he cited some examples of the antithesis, as a contrast. One that is worth noting is the idea of leadership by a star. There's more than one defect in the concept of leadership by a star. First of all, of course, it doesn't build a team; building of a team, in the last analysis, is the development of the widest possible leadership. In that way you've got as much hitting power as you can have in the cumulative leadership structure of the party, from the central leaders on down to the various levels of the organization. There's another defect in the leadership of a star. An organizer should be able to have everybody active. If there's somebody in a branch who isn't contributing to the party in the way they could, it means that the given organizer, who is responsible for that person's activities, is not wholly doing his or her job. One of the criteria for an organizer is to get production, activity, contributions from each member of the party. Now a leader who plays the role of a star is generally able to activate people only to the extent that they can be used in a specific activity where the leader is out scintillating. If you can't be used for this star's particular caper at the given moment, he or she doesn't know what to do with you.

A second contrast that Comrade Cannon cited was the notion of having cliquists as leaders. I think enough has already been said here about cliques, so I don't need to elaborate on that.

Another contrast he cites is the leadership of a cult. He took the example of Johnson, who was the leader of the state capitalist tendency in the American Trotskyist movement. But we also had others. There were two or three varieties of cultists in the organized minorities of the late 1950s and early 1960s. One was the present leader of the Workers World-YAWF grouping, Sam Marcy. Sometimes you get the feeling he has a messianic complex. In any event, he leads by the method of a cult. A cult is like a religion—"there is only one true god—me!!! If you don't believe it, then you are an infidel. And if you try to do something about it, there's the door." That's the attitude of the cult leader. We had another cultist out in Milwaukee, James Boulton. In addition to being a cult leader, he was a poet, and a machine worker whose throw was off. But he supported the Swabeck tendency in the dispute of the 1960s on the Chinese question. After he left the party, he joined up with the cult leader Marcy. The irresistible force and the immovable object came together in the same organization, and we soon found out that the immovable object wasn't immovable. Some of Marcy's henchmen went up to Milwaukee and physically threw Boulton out of his own headquarters. That settled that question.

Now let's come back to the idea of a team leadership. The object of team leadership is to build the kind of a leadership formation that is so linked to the ranks of the party, and so representative of the party because of the standing that the collective leaders have as a team, that the leaders can carry the movement through the stresses and strains, the ups and downs, the twists and turns that go with the total process of revolutionary activity, without throwing the movement into convulsions. There's a rapport, a liaison, a real affinity between the leadership and the ranks. That must be one quality of a team.

Within the team itself, there has to be objectivity,

---

* "Factional Struggle and Party Leadership" can be found in Cannon's *Speeches to the Party*

mutual respect, a sense of mutual responsibility, a common understanding of the role of leadership in the party, a very extensive area of agreement on the essentials of the program, the strategy, and the tactics of the party, and a capacity to sort out the relative weight of things.

A member of a branch executive committee, working within the framework of a team concept, should keep two things in mind. One is that if he or she has a difference of opinion, with a majority of the branch executive committee, then under the principles of democratic centralism, that individual has the right to go to the branch with a minority report on the question. But a second thing that same individual should keep in mind is that a leader should not act impetuously.

I mentioned already that a leader can't wear two coats, one in the capacity of a leader, and the other in the capacity of an individual. If you take on a leadership responsibility, and if you're going to be a leader worth a tinker's dam, you automatically have to give up part of your rights as an individual. You can't have it both ways. You can't be a foot-loose, fancy-free rank and filer and a leader at the same time. It just won't work. If you've taken any kind of leading position, you've got to think, not only about your own opinion, but also about the organization. You must have a sense of proportion. A comrade with a dissident view in the executive committee has got to say to himself or herself, "Well, I still think I'm right, but is this question of such a magnitude that I ought to go in to the branch meeting against the rest of the executive committee, and make a minority report, and have a big argument in the branch?" Maybe you should, maybe you shouldn't. I'm not saying one or the other. But think about it, be conscious of it, and remember that a leader, at whatever level, in whatever function, is responsible not only for the correct programmatic strategic and tactical line of the party, or the given unit of the party in its work, but also for the equilibrium of the party, or of that party unit. It's a damn poor stick of a leader who is always keeping the organization in a state of turmoil by constantly raising objections and minority views over small questions. If you do that, you will also discredit yourself in the eyes of the ranks. It will get to be like that old fable about the kid who called wolf. If you quibble over every little question that comes up, and then one day a serious question comes up that you want to raise, and you will have made such a nuisance of yourself that nobody will pay any attention to you.

So a team leadership must be grounded in a firm relation between the leadership and the unit that is led, on the basis of confidence in and respect for the leading unit by the comrades in the ranks. There must be a relationship of mutual respect and recognition of the responsibilities of leadership among the comrades working in the leadership team. And, the individual members of that team must have a sense of proportion about going to the party with differences of opinion that may develop within the team.

Now, just one final point on that that has to do with leadership. I spoke earlier about the danger of an organized minority artificially perpetuating itself as an organized formation inside the party after the given issue has been voted on and settled. Such a minority runs the risk of degenerating into a clique. This applies also to the problem of leaders functioning with respect to a team concept in leadership. The situation that is most conducive to building a team is when each leader has the understanding and capacity to stand in an undifferentiated relationship with the other members of the leadership, and with all members of the party. You have no special relation with any other particular leader, or any particular member or group of members inside the party.

If a difference of opinion arises, and a dispute develops, then it may be necessary temporarily to have some differentiated organizational associations within the leadership. It may be necessary for one grouping to join together collectively in thinking out the points of view that it might want to express as against the points of view of another grouping. But as soon as that issue is settled, then the organized formation should be dissolved. If a leader tries artificially to perpetuate a grouping within the party, that can develop into cliquism.

QUESTION: If factions are so dangerous, shouldn't the party outlaw factions in its constitution? Also, does a minority tendency have the automatic right to proportional representation in the leadership?

ANSWER: Let's take up the question about factions first.

There was one juncture in the history of the Bolshevik Party where they did suppress the right of factions. It was at the most extreme point in an exceedingly dangerous civil war, where they were confronted by massive imperialist intervention. In those circumstances, for that given juncture, under the exigencies of the struggle of that moment, Lenin and Trotsky lent themselves to proscribing factions temporarily—but only temporarily, and only under these circumstances. I won't attempt here to pass judgment on that decision because it is a question that requires much thought and explanation. I should add, however, that there has since been much consideration in the revolutionary movement as to whether that decision was justified, even under those extreme circumstances, because it helped to give some simulacrum of a political justification to the Stalinists for making it a standard policy later, for strictly bureaucratic reasons.

The essence of Leninism includes the right to organize factions and tendencies. Now, as I have tried to point out here, it is best if comrades are mature enough and understanding enough to handle a difference of opinion through the organization of an ideological tendency. That entails the minimum danger of generating convulsive internal conditions, which are always implicit in the formation of a faction. But it would be wrong to suppress the right of organizing a faction, because the political differences may be so deep that a faction is necessary.

The question can also be looked at from this point of view. There is always a danger of split when a faction develops. But splits are also necessary at times. In addition to the molecular process of individual recruitment, a party is also built through a combined process of unifications and splits. Oftentimes splits accompany unifications.

Let me give you one example from the history of our movement. In the spring of 1936, when we were getting ready to enter the Socialist Party, we had a minority in the party headed by Hugo Oehler, who was a sectarian. Oehler was dead set against the entry into the SP. He made a principle out of the idea that the party had to be exactly as it was, with its name as it was then, the Workers Party, which couldn't be changed. He organized a faction, a heated factional struggle ensued, and a split took place. Oehler organized his faction because he felt that the course the party was proposing to take would lead to the end of the Trotskyist movement. He thought he had to try and save as much of the party as he could, and take the leadership of the party himself. So, simultaneous with our entry into the SP in 1936, we had the split of the sectarians led by Oehler. But if we had proscribed the right of factions, what would have happened? Nothing would have changed politically. These sectarians would have retained the attitude they had, they would have pursued the course they pursued, only in a different way, one which could have disrupted the entire entry tactic. But with the right of organization of factions inside the party, we had the mechanism to deal with these sectarians, and we were able to resolve the question in the best way for the party.

When a revolutionary party functions in the hostile environment of capitalist society, there are many pressures that generate dissidence in the ranks. From time to time the party goes through processes of purge. In the course of a fight, you more deeply assimilate those who have the capacity to identify with the revolutionary movement, and the party tends to throw off other elements who have not proven to be assimilable. The organization of internal conflict is an important vehicle in this regard.

It is a matter of the most extreme importance, to a revolutionary combat party, and it is basic to democratic centralist concepts, that the right of organized dissent be protected within the party. While it is true that a faction tends to develop its own program and its own discipline, and that it implies war on the party, and it implies a split, if the party is not able to handle itself despite that, it means that something is wrong with the party leadership. If you can't handle it, don't outlaw factions, don't outlaw tendencies, but change the leadership. Get a leadership that knows what it is doing.

Now, on the question of proportional representation. There are two aspects to this question. First, as Lenin taught, it is in the best interests of the majority leadership of the party to have representatives of minority tendencies within the leadership. They reflect a certain component of one or another magnitude, within the ranks of the party. By having representatives of a minority tendency within the leadership, it is possible for the leadership as a whole to keep more in touch with the climate in the party. It can proceed in the most informed, careful and responsible way with regard to divergences of view that may exist within the party, and the impact this has on the good and welfare of the party as a whole. From that point of view, a leadership that knows its Leninism will always be sensitive and attentive to giving minorities representation in the leadership.

That's one aspect of this question. There is also another. *The minority has to be loyal to the party.* Here I'll give you another example. At the 1963 convention of the SWP, Wohlforth and Robertson were both leaders of minority factions within the party. The nominating commission brought in a recommendation to the convention that they *not* be included on the incoming National Committee. This was debated before the convention, and the convention voted in its overwhelming majority that they should *not* be. Why? Because their loyalty to the party was in question. If we had made a mechanical provision that a minority is automatically entitled to proportional representation in the leading bodies of the party, we could get into some binds that are contrary to the interests of the party.

The best way to put it is to say that we generally give loyal minorities representation on the leading bodies of the party. This need not necessarily be a strictly proportional representation, however. Take the example of the developing split with the petty bourgeois opposition of 1939–1940. The majority was not much over 50%. The party was split almost right down the middle. So, at the 1939 party convention, when the National Committee elected the Political Committee for the next period, it deliberately weighted it with a majority in excess of the actual majority percentage within the party as a whole. The reason was to prevent a situation in which the representatives of the party minority could get an accidental majority at a given meeting of the PC. If we had elected a PC only narrowly divided between the majority and the minority, suppose that a member of the majority was sick, and another was out on tour or on an assignment someplace. A minority might accidentally become a temporary majority and try to take advantage of that situation. What a ludicrous thing that would be.

Appendix

NATIONAL COMMITTEE PLENUM RESOLUTION ON THE ORGANIZATIONAL PRINCIPLES OF THE PARTY

Note: The following resolution was unanimously adopted by the May 1953 plenum of the National Committee of the Socialist Workers Party. It includes previous SWP resolutions passed in 1938 and 1940. These resolutions are superseded by a resolution passed at the 21st National Convention of the Socialist Workers Party held in September 1965. The 1965 resolution is available in an Education for Socialists Bulletin. It is entitled "The Organizational Character of the Socialist Workers Party."

I

The Plenum of the National Committee reaffirms the resolution adopted by the 1938 Founding Convention of the Socialist Workers Party "On the Internal Situation and the Character of the Party," as follows (except that any reference indicating or implying affiliation with the Fourth International is no longer valid in view of the fact that the Socialist Workers Party formally disaffiliated from the Fourth International in 1940 because of the anti-democratic Voorhis Act):

"The Socialist Workers Party is a revolutionary Marxian party, based on a definite program, whose aim is the organization of the working class in the struggle for power and the transformation of the existing social order. All of its activities, its methods and its internal regime are subordinated to this aim and are designed to serve it.

"Only a self-acting and critical-minded membership is capable of forging and consolidating such a party and of solving its problems by collective thought, discussion and experience. From this follows the need of assuring the widest party democracy in the ranks of the organization.

"The struggle for power organized and led by the revolutionary party is the most ruthless and irreconcilable struggle in all history. A loosely-knit, heterogeneous, undisciplined, untrained organization is utterly incapable of accomplishing such world-historical tasks as the proletariat and the revolutionary party are confronted with in the present era. This is all the more emphatically true in the light of the singularly difficult position of our party and the extraordinary persecution to which it is subject. From this follows the party's unconditional demand upon all its members for complete discipline in all the public activities and actions of the organization.

"Leadership and centralized direction are indispensable prerequisites for any sustained and disciplined action, especially in the party that sets for itself the aim of leading the collective efforts of the proletariat in its struggle against capitalism. Without a strong and firm Central Committee, having the power to act promptly and effectively in the name of the party and to supervise, coordinate and direct all its activities without exception, the very idea of a revolutionary party is a meaningless jest.

"It is from these considerations, based upon the whole of the experience of working class struggle throughout the world in the last century, that we derive the Leninist principle of organization, namely democratic centralism. The same experience has demonstrated that there are no absolute guarantees for the preservation of the principle of democratic centralism, and no rigid formula that can be set down in advance, a priori, for the application of it under any and all circumstances. Proceeding from certain fundamental conceptions, the problem of applying the principle of democratic centralism differently under different conditions and stages of development of the struggle, can be solved only in relation to the concrete situation, in the course of the tests and experience through which the movement passes, and on the basis of the most fruitful and healthy inter-relationship of the leading bodies of the party and its rank and file.

'The responsibilities of leadership'

"The leadership of the party must be under the control of the membership, its policies must always be open to criticism, discussion and rectification by the rank and file within properly established forms and limits, and the leading bodies themselves subject to formal recall or alteration. The membership of the party has the right to demand and expect the greatest responsibility from the leaders precisely because of the position they occupy in the movement. The selection of comrades to the positions of leadership means the conferring of an extraordinary responsibility. The warrant for this position must be proved, not once, but continuously by the leadership itself. It is under obligation to set the highest example of responsibility, devotion, sacrifice and complete identification with the party itself and its daily life and action. It must display the ability to defend its policies before the membership of the party, and to defend the line of the party and the party as a whole before the working class in general.

"Sustained party activity, not broken or disrupted by abrupt and disorienting changes, presupposes not only a continuity of tradition and a systematic development of party policy, but also the continuity of leadership. It is an important sign of a serious and firmly constituted party, of a party really engaged in productive work in the class struggle, that it throws up out of its ranks cadres of more or less able leading comrades, tested for their qualities of endurance and trustworthiness, and that it thus insures a certain stability and continuity of leadership by such a cadre.

"Continuity of leadership does not, however, signify the automatic self-perpetuation of leadership. Constant renewal of its ranks by means of additions and, when necessary, replacements, is the only assurance that the party has, that its leadership will not succumb to the effects of dry-rot, that it will not be burdened with deadwood, that it will avoid the corrosion of conservatism and dilettantism, that it will not be the object of conflict between the older elements and the younger, that the old and basic cadre will be refreshed by new blood, that the leadership as a whole will not become purely bureaucratic 'committee men' with a life that is remote from the real life of the party and the activities of the rank and file.

'Responsibilities of membership'

"Like leadership, membership itself in the party implies certain definite rights. Party membership confers the fullest freedom of discussion, debate and criticism inside the ranks of the party, limited only by such decisions and provisions as are made by the party itself or by bodies to which it assigns this function. Affiliation to the party confers upon each member the right of being democratically represented at all policy-making assemblies of the party (from branch to national and international convention), and the right of the final and decisive vote in determining the program, policies and leadership of the party.

"With party rights, the membership has also certain definite obligations. The theoretical and political character of the party is determined by its program, which forms the lines delimiting the revolutionary party from all other parties, groups and tendencies in the working class. The first obligation of party membership is loyal acceptance of the program of the party and regular affiliation to one of the basic units of the party. The party requires of every member the acceptance of its discipline and the carrying on of his activity in accordance with the program of the party, with the decisions adopted by its conventions, and with the policies formulated and directed by the party leadership.

"Party membership implies the obligation of one hundred per cent loyalty to the organization, the rejection of all agents of other, hostile groups in its ranks, and intolerance of divided loyalties in general. Membership in the party necessitates a minimum of activity in the organization, as established by the proper unit, and under the direction of the party; it necessitates the fulfillment of all the tasks which the party assigns to each member. Party membership implies the obligation upon every member to contribute materially to the support of the organization in accordance with his means.

'A party of revolutionary workers'

"From the foregoing it follows that the party seeks to include in its ranks all the revolutionary, class conscious and militant workers who stand on its program and are active in building the movement in a disciplined manner. The revolutionary Marxian party rejects not only the arbitrariness and bureaucratism of the Communist Party, but also the spurious and deceptive 'all-inclusiveness' of the Thomas-Tyler-Hoan Socialist Party, which is a sham and a fraud. Experience has proved conclusively that this 'all-inclusiveness' paralyzes the party in general and the revolutionary left wing in particular, suppressing and bureaucratically hounding the latter while giving free rein to the right wing to commit the greatest crimes in the name of socialism and the party. The SWP seeks to be inclusive only in this sense: that it accepts into its ranks those who accept its program and denies admission to those who reject its program.

"The rights of each individual member, as set forth above, do not imply that the membership as a whole, namely, the party itself, does not possess rights of its own. The party as a whole has the right to demand that its work be not disrupted and disorganized, and has the right to take all the measures which it finds necessary to assure its regular and normal functioning. The rights of any individual member are distinctly secondary to the rights of the party membership as a whole. Party democracy means not only the most scrupulous protection of the rights of a given minority, but also the protection of the rule of the majority. The party is therefore entitled to organize the discussion and to determine its forms and limits.

"All inner-party discussion must be organized from the point of view that the party is not a discussion club which debates interminably on any and all questions at any and all times, without arriving at a binding decision that enables the organization to act, but from the point of view that we are a disciplined party of revolutionary action. The party in general not only has the right, therefore, to organize the discussion in accordance with the requirements of the situation, but the lower units of the party must be given the right, in the interests of the struggle against the disruption and disorganization of the party's work, to call irresponsible individuals to order and, if need be, to eject them from the ranks.

"The decisions of the national party convention are binding on all party members without exception and they conclude the discussion on all these disputed questions upon which a decision has been taken. Any party member violating the decisions of the convention, or attempting to revive discussion in regard to them without formal authorization of the party, puts himself thereby in opposition to the party and forfeits his right to membership. All party organizations are authorized and instructed to take any measures necessary to enforce this rule."

II

The Plenum of the National Committee reaffirms the resolution adopted by the 1940 Convention of the SWP on "The Organizational Conclusions of the Present Discussion," as follows (except that any reference indicating or implying affiliation with the Fourth International is no longer valid in view of the fact that the Socialist Workers Party formally disaffiliated from the Fourth International in 1940 because of the anti-democratic Voorhis Act):

"The Bolshevik party of Lenin is the only party in history which successfully conquered and held state power. The SWP, as a combat organization, which aims at achieving power in this country, models its organization forms and methods after those of the Russian Bolshevik party, adapting them, naturally, to the experience of recent years and to concrete American conditions.

"The SWP as a revolutionary workers' party is based on the doctrines of scientific socialism as embodied in the principal works of Marx, Engels, Lenin and Trotsky and incorporated in the basic documents and resolutions of the first four congresses of the Communist International and of the conferences and congresses of the Fourth International.

"The SWP rejects the contention of social democrats, skeptics and capitulators disillusioned in the Russian revolution, that there is an inevitable and organic connection between Bolshevism and Stalinism. This reactionary revision of Marxism is a capitulation to democratic imperialism. It is capable of producing only demoralization and defeat in the critical times of war and revolution.

"The rise of reaction on a world scale, accompanied and produced by the disastrous course of Stalinism in the working class movement, has catapulted all centrist groups and parties (Lovestoneites, Socialist Party, London Bureau) away from Bolshevism and in the direction of social democracy. In whole or in part, all of these groups attempt to identify Bolshevism with Stalinism. Without exception these groups are all in a state of collapse and passing over to the side of the class enemy.

'Petty bourgeoisie transmits skepticism'
"This tendency (Souvarinism) has manifested itself in leading circles of our party (Burnham) and in certain sections of the membership. Their skeptical criticisms of Bolshevism express their petty-bourgeois composition and their dependence on bourgeois public opinion. The petty bourgeoisie is a natural transmission belt carrying the theories of reaction into the organizations of the working class.

"Those who seek to identify Bolshevism with Stalinism concern themselves with a search for guarantees against the Stalinist degeneration of the party and the future Soviet power. We reject this demand for insurance as completely un-dialectical and unrealistic. Our party, in the first instance, is concerned with the struggle for state power, and therefore with creating a party organization capable of leading the proletarian struggle to this goal. There are no constitutional guarantees which can prevent degeneration. Only the victorious revolution can provide the necessary preconditions for preventing the degeneration of the party and the future Soviet power. If the party fails to carry through and extend the revolution the degeneration of the party is inevitable.

"Insofar as any guarantees are possible against the degeneration of the proletarian party, these can be obtained only by educating the party in firm adherence to principles and by a merciless struggle against all personal and unprincipled clique combinations within the party. The outstanding example of this clique formation is the Abern group which is based solely on personal loyalties and on rewards of honor and place within the party for those whose primary loyalty is to the clique. The history of the Fourth International in this country amply reveals that such a clique, with its utter disregard for principles, can become the repository for alien class influences and agents of enemy organizations seeking to disrupt the Fourth International from within. The SWP condemns the Abern clique as hostile to the spirit and methods of Bolshevik organization.

'Revolutionary centralism'
"To overthrow the most powerful capitalist ruling class in the world, the SWP must be organized as a combat party on strong centralist lines. The resolution adopted at the founding convention gave a correct interpretation of the principle of democratic centralism. Its emphasis was placed on the democratic aspects of this principle. The party leadership has faithfully preserved the democratic rights of the membership since the founding convention. It has granted the widest latitude of discussion to all dissenting groups and individuals. The duty of the incoming National Committee is to execute the decisions of the convention, arrived at after the most thorough and democratic discussion, and to permit no infringement upon them.

"Conditions, both external and in the internal development of the party, demand that steps now be taken towards knitting the party together, towards tightening up its activities and centralizing its organization structure. For the work of penetrating into the workers' mass movement, for the heavy struggles to come against capitalism, for the onerous conditions of war, it is imperative that a maximum of loyalty be required of every leader and every member, that a maximum of activity be required, that a strict adherence to discipline be demanded and rigidly enforced.

'The press'
"The party press is the decisive public agitational and propagandist expression of the Bolshevik organization. The policies of the press are formulated on the basis of the fundamental resolutions of the congresses and conferences of the International, the conventions of the party, the decisions of the National Committee not in conflict with such resolutions. Control of the press is lodged directly in the hands of the National Committee by the convention of the party. The duty of the editors is loyally to interpret the decisions of the convention in the press.

'Control of public discussion'
"The opening of the party press to discussion of a point of view contrary to that of the official leader-

ship of the party or of its programmatic convention decisions must be controlled by the National Committee which is obligated to regulate discussion of this character in such a way as to give decisive emphasis to the party line. It is the right and duty of the National Committee to veto any demand for public discussion if it deems such discussion harmful to the best interests of the party.

"The petty-bourgeois opposition in our party demonstrates its hostility to Bolshevik organization by its demand that the minority be granted the right to transform the press into a discussion organ for diametrically opposite programs. By that method it would take the control of the press out of the hands of the National Committee and subordinate it to any temporary, anarchistic combination which can make itself heard at the moment.

"By the same token, the demand of the petty-bourgeois opposition for an independent public organ, expounding a program in opposition to that of the majority of the party, represents a complete abandonment of democratic centralism and a capitulation to the Norman Thomas type of 'all-inclusive' party which is inclusive of all tendencies except the Bolshevik. The granting of this demand for a separate organ would destroy the centralist character of the party, by creating dual central committees, dual editorial boards, dual treasuries, dual distribution agencies, divided loyalties and a complete breakdown of all discipline. Under such conditions the party would rapidly degenerate into a social democratic organization or disappear from the scene altogether. The convention categorically rejects the demand for a dual organ.

'Leadership'

"To build the combat organization capable of conquering state power, the party must have as its general staff a corps of professional revolutionists who devote their entire life to the direction and the building of the party and its influence in the mass movement. Membership in the leading staff of the party, the National Committee, must be made contingent on a complete subordination of the life of the candidate to the party. All members of the National Committee must devote full-time activities to party work, or be prepared to do so at the demand of the National Committee.

"In the struggle for power, the party demands the greatest sacrifices of its members. Only a leadership selected from among those who demonstrate in the struggle the qualities of singleness of purpose, unconditional loyalty to the party and revolutionary firmness of character, can inspire the membership with a spirit of unswerving devotion and lead the party in its struggle for power.

"The party leadership must, from time to time, be infused with new blood, primarily from its proletarian sections. Workers who show promise and ability through activity in the union movement and its strike struggle should be elevated to the leading committees of the party in order to establish a more direct connection between the leading committee and the workers' movement, and in order to train the worker-Bolshevik for the task of party direction itself.

"The party must select from its younger members those qualified, talented and promising elements who can be trained for leadership. The road of the student youth to the party leadership must not and cannot be from the classroom of the high school and college directly into the leading committee. They must first prove themselves. They must be sent without high-sounding titles into working class districts for day-to-day work among the proletariat. The young student must serve an apprenticeship in the workers' movement before he can be considered as candidate for the National Committee.

'Proletarianize the party'

"The working class is the only class in modern society that is progressive and truly revolutionary. Only the working class is capable of saving humanity from barbarism. Only a revolutionary party can lead the proletariat to the realization of this historic mission. To achieve power, the revolutionary party must be deeply rooted among the workers, it must be composed predominantly of workers and enjoy the respect and confidence of the workers.

"Without such a composition it is impossible to build a programmatically firm and disciplined organization which can accomplish these grandiose tasks. A party of non-workers is necessarily subject to all the reactionary influences of skepticism, cynicism, soul-sickness and capitulatory despair transmitted to it through its petty-bourgeois environment.

"To transform the SWP into a proletarian party of action, particularly in the present period of reaction, it is not enough to continue propagandistic activities in the hope that by an automatic process workers will flock to the banner of the party. It is necessary, on the contrary, to make a concerted, determined and systematic effort, consciously directed by the leading committees of the party, to penetrate the workers' movement, establish the roots of the party in the trade unions, the mass labor organizations and in the workers' neighborhoods and recruit worker militants into the ranks of the party.

'Steps to proletarianize the party'

"To proletarianize the party, the following steps are imperative:

"1. The entire party membership must be directed towards rooting itself in the factories, mills, etc., and towards integrating itself in the unions and workers' mass organizations.

"2. Those members of the party who are not workers shall be assigned to work in labor organizations, in workers' neighborhoods and with the worker-fractions of the party—to assist them and learn from them. All unemployed members must belong to and be active in organizations of the unemployed.

"*Those party members who find it impossible after a reasonable period of time to work in a proletarian milieu and to attract to the party worker militants shall be transferred from party membership to the rank of sympathizers. Special organizations of sympathizers may be formed for this purpose.*

"Above all the student and unemployed youth must be sent into industry and involved in the life and struggles of the workers. Systematic, exceptional and persistent efforts must be made to assist the integration of our unemployed youth into industry despite the restricted field of employment.

"Lacking connection with the workers' movement through failure or inability to get jobs in industry or membership in unions, the student and unemployed youth are subject to terrific pressure from the petty-bourgeois world. A large section of the youth membership of the SWP and YPSL adopted the program of the Fourth International, but brought with them the training and habits of the social democratic movement, which are far removed from the spirit of the proletarian revolution.

"These student elements can transform the program of the Fourth International from the pages of books and pamphlets into living reality for themselves and for the party only by integrating themselves in the workers' movement and breaking irrevocably from their previous environment. Unless they follow this road they are in constant danger of slipping back into their former social democratic habits or into complete apathy and pessimism and thus be lost for the revolutionary movement.

"3. To attract and to hold workers in the ranks of the party, it is necessary that the internal life of the party be drastically transformed. The party must be cleansed of the discussion club atmosphere, of an irresponsible attitude toward assignments, of a cynical and smart-aleck disrespect for the party.

'Organizing real campaigns'

"Party activity must be lifted out of dragging, daily routine and reorganized on the basis of campaigns which are realistically adjusted to the demands and direction of the workers' movement. These campaigns must not be sucked out of the thumb of some functionary in a party office, but must arise as a result of the connections of the party with the workers' movement and the indicated direction of the masses in specific situations.

"All party agitation campaigns, especially in the next period, must be directed primarily at those workers' groups and organizations in which we are attempting to gain a foothold and attract members. General agitation addressed to the working class as a whole or the public in general must be related to those specific aims.

"The press must gear its agitation into the activity conducted among specific workers' groups so as to transform the party paper from a literary organ into a workers' organizer. The integration of the party into the workers' movement, and the transformation of the party into a proletarian organization, are indispensable for the progress of the party. Successful achievement of this internal transformation is a thousand times more important than any amount of empty phrases about 'preparation of the party for war.' This transformation is, in fact, the only real preparation of the party for war, combined of course with the necessary technical adjustments in organization forms.

"The SWP must adhere to the principles and program of the Fourth International, transform itself into a democratically centralized Bolshevik organization, integrate itself into the workers' movement. On that basis, and on that basis alone, can the party meet the test of the war, survive the war and go forward to its great goal—the establishment of a Workers' Republic in the United States."

III

The Plenum of the National Committee reaffirms as follows the organizational principles and procedures of the party:

As provided by the party constitution, the National Committee directs all the work of the party, decides all questions of policy in accord with the decisions of the national convention, appoints subordinate officers and subcommittees, including the Political Committee, and in general constitutes, between national conventions, the functioning central authority of the party.

The Political Committee, appointed by the plenum, functions as the central authority of the party between plenums of the National Committee and is authorized to speak and act in its name. It shall be optional with the Political Committee whether or not it will conduct a poll of the National Committee before acting on any question before it, except that such a poll shall be taken upon the request of any National Committee member for a plenary meeting of the National Committee. The Political Committee is obliged to comply with the decision of the full National Committee in such a poll.

All party organs, institutions and bodies, including the party locals and branches, shall be under the supervision of the Political Committee, acting for the National Committee. All party units and individual party members are required to comply with any directives of the Political Committee between plenums of the National Committee, pending appeal to the plenum.

As provided by the party constitution, Local Executive Committees shall direct the activities of the Locals and act with full power for the Locals between city conventions. Branch Executive Committees, on the other hand, as provided by the party constitution, shall be subordinate to the Branch membership.

In accordance with the principle of democratic centralism, the minority shall have the right to present its views in the internal party discussion. The plenum, and between its sessions the Political Committee, has the right and duty to lay down rules for the regulation of the discussion, to see that it is fairly conducted as has invariably been the case in the past, and to see that it does not disrupt party work and the orderly functioning of the party in all its activities.

The principle of majority rule shall apply with full force and effect in all party bodies, and in all party activities.

Workers and the US rulers' deepening political crisis

Three books for today's spreading and deepening debate among working people looking for a way forward in face of capitalism's global economic and social calamity and wars.

Are They Rich Because They're Smart?
Class, privilege, and learning under capitalism
JACK BARNES

Also in Spanish, French, Farsi, and Arabic.
$10.

The Clintons' Anti-Working-Class Record
Why Washington fears working people
JACK BARNES

Also in Spanish, French, Farsi, and Greek.
$10.

Is Socialist Revolution in the US Possible?
A necessary debate among working people
MARY-ALICE WATERS

Also in Spanish, French, and Farsi.
$7.

RELATED READINGS

The Transitional Program for Socialist Revolution
LEON TROTSKY

The Socialist Workers Party program, drafted by Trotsky in 1938, still guides the SWP and communists the world over. The party "uncompromisingly gives battle to all political groupings tied to the apron strings of the bourgeoisie. Its task—the abolition of capitalism's domination. Its aim—socialism. Its method—the proletarian revolution."

Also in Farsi.
$17.

Capitalism's World Disorder
Working-class politics at the millennium
JACK BARNES

The social devastation and financial panic, coarsening of politics, cop brutality, and imperialist aggression—all are products not of something gone wrong with capitalism but of its lawful workings. Yet the future can be changed by the united struggle of workers and farmers increasingly conscious of their capacity to wage revolutionary struggles for state power and to transform the world.

Also in Spanish and French.
$20.

WWW.PATHFINDERPRESS.COM

COMMUNIST CONTINUITY AND PROGRAM

Labor, Nature, and the Evolution of Humanity
The Long View of History
FREDERICK ENGELS, KARL MARX
GEORGE NOVACK
MARY-ALICE WATERS

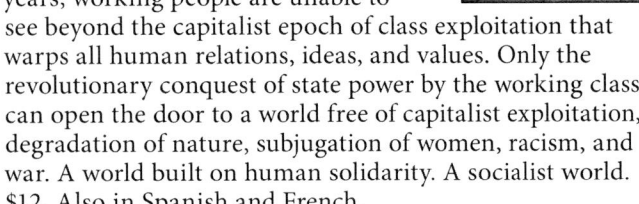

Without understanding that social labor, transforming nature, has driven humanity's evolution for millions of years, working people are unable to see beyond the capitalist epoch of class exploitation that warps all human relations, ideas, and values. Only the revolutionary conquest of state power by the working class can open the door to a world free of capitalist exploitation, degradation of nature, subjugation of women, racism, and war. A world built on human solidarity. A socialist world. $12. Also in Spanish and French.

The Communist Manifesto
KARL MARX AND FREDERICK ENGELS

Communism, say the founding leaders of the revolutionary workers movement, is not a set of ideas or preconceived "principles" but workers' line of march to power, springing from a "movement going on under our very eyes." $5. Also in Spanish, French, Farsi, and Arabic.

Their Trotsky and Ours
JACK BARNES

To lead the working class in a successful revolution, a mass proletarian party is needed whose cadres, well beforehand, have absorbed a world communist program, are proletarian in life and work, derive deep satisfaction from doing politics, and have forged a leadership with an acute sense of what to do next. This book is about building such a party. $12. Also in Spanish, French, and Farsi.

Socialism on Trial
Testimony at Minneapolis Sedition Trial
JAMES P. CANNON

The revolutionary program of the working class, presented in response to frame-up charges of "seditious conspiracy" in 1941, on the eve of US entry into World War II. The defendants were leaders of the Minneapolis labor movement and the Socialist Workers Party. $15. Also in Spanish, French, and Farsi.

The Low Point of Labor Resistance Is Behind Us
The Socialist Workers Party Looks Forward
JACK BARNES, MARY-ALICE WATERS
STEVE CLARK

The global order imposed by victors of the inter-imperialist slaughter of World War II is shattering, with explosive ramifications for workers and farmers worldwide. A long retreat by the working class and unions has come to an end. More and more workers of all ages, skin colors, and both sexes are saying, "Enough is enough!" This book highlights opportunities ahead for class-conscious workers to forge a labor party built on the unions. And a mass proletarian vanguard able to lead the struggle to end capitalist rule, opening a future for humanity. $10. Also in Spanish and French.

Revolutionary Continuity
Marxist Leadership in the U.S.
The Early Years, 1848–1917
Birth of the Communist Movement, 1918–1922
FARRELL DOBBS

"Successive generations of proletarian revolutionists have participated in the movements of the working class and its allies.... Marxists today owe them not only homage for their deeds. We also have a duty to learn what they did wrong as well as right so their errors are not repeated." —*Farrell Dobbs*. Two volumes, $17 each.

The Third International after Lenin
LEON TROTSKY

Leon Trotsky's 1928 defense of the Marxist course that had guided the Communist International in its early years. Writing in the heat of political battle, Trotsky addresses the key challenge facing working people today: building communist parties throughout the world capable of leading workers and farmers to take power. $20. Also in Farsi.

Cuba and the Coming American Revolution
JACK BARNES

This is a book about the struggles of working people in the imperialist heartland, the youth attracted to them, and the example set by the Cuban people that revolution is not only necessary—it can be made. It is about the class struggle in the US, where the revolutionary capacities of workers and farmers are today as utterly discounted by the ruling powers as were those of the Cuban toilers. And just as wrongly. $10. Also in Spanish, French, and Farsi.

Opening Guns of World War III: Washington's Assault on Iraq
JACK BARNES

The murderous assault on Iraq in 1990–91 heralded increasingly sharp conflicts among imperialist powers, growing instability of capitalism, and more wars. Also includes:

1945: When US Troops Said No! by Mary-Alice Waters

Lessons from the Iran-Iraq War by Samad Sharif

In *New International* no. 7. $14. Also in Spanish, French, and Farsi.

The Revolution Betrayed
What Is the Soviet Union and Where Is It Going?
LEON TROTSKY

In 1917 workers and peasants of Russia were the motor force for one of the deepest revolutions in history. Yet within ten years a political counterrevolution by a privileged social layer, whose chief spokesperson was Joseph Stalin, was being consolidated. The classic study of the Soviet workers state and its degeneration. $17. Also in Spanish, Farsi, and Greek.

Background to 'The Struggle for a Proletarian Party'
GEORGE CLARKE, JAMES P. CANNON, LEON TROTSKY

The challenges faced by the Socialist Workers Party in deepening its involvement in the organizations and struggles of the industrial working class in the years prior to US imperialism's entry into World War II. The SWP must "orient in practice the whole organization toward the factories, the strikes, the unions," writes Leon Trotsky in a 1937 letter to party leader James P. Cannon. $5

Colombia: Fidel Castro on the Debate around Revolutionary Strategy and Lessons of the Cuban Revolution
FROM THE PAGES OF THE *MILITANT*

Excerpts from Fidel Castro's *Peace in Colombia* and articles from the *Militant*. In describing the Cuban leadership's efforts to end decades of war between the FARC guerrilla movement and Colombia's brutal regime, Castro in his prologue, afterword, and other statements explains why Cuban revolutionaries, unlike FARC leaders, rejected taking hostages and organized working people to win state power, not pursue a "prolonged people's war." $5. Also in Spanish.

In Defense of the US Working Class
MARY-ALICE WATERS

Drawing on the fighting traditions of the oppressed and exploited of all colors and national origins, in 2018 tens of thousands of teachers and other working people in West Virginia, Oklahoma, and other states waged victorious strikes. They fought for dignity and respect for themselves, their families, and for all working people. $7. Also in Spanish, French, Farsi, and Greek.

Lenin's Final Fight
Speeches and Writings, 1922–23
V.I. LENIN

In 1922 and 1923, V.I. Lenin, central leader of the world's first socialist revolution, waged what was to be his last political battle—one that was lost following his death. At stake was whether that revolution, and the international communist movement it led, would remain on the revolutionary proletarian course that brought workers and peasants to power in October 1917. $17. Also in Spanish, Farsi, and Greek.

The Struggle for a Proletarian Party
JAMES P. CANNON

"The workers of America have power enough to topple the structure of capitalism at home and to lift the whole world with them when they rise," Cannon asserts. On the eve of World War II, a founder of the communist movement in the US and leader of the Communist International in Lenin's time defends the program and party-building norms of Bolshevism. $20. Also in Spanish and Farsi.

WWW.PATHFINDERPRESS.COM

EXPAND YOUR REVOLUTIONARY LIBRARY

Imperialism's March toward Fascism and War
JACK BARNES

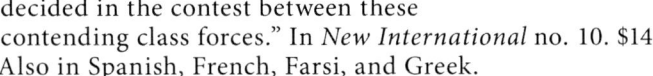

"There will be new Hitlers, new Mussolinis. That is inevitable. What is not inevitable is that they will triumph. The working-class vanguard will organize our class to fight back against the devastating toll we are made to pay for the capitalist crisis. The future of humanity will be decided in the contest between these contending class forces." In *New International* no. 10. $14. Also in Spanish, French, Farsi, and Greek.

In Defense of Marxism
Against the Petty-Bourgeois Opposition in the Socialist Workers Party
LEON TROTSKY

A reply to those in the revolutionary workers movement in the late 1930s bending to bourgeois patriotism during Washington's buildup to enter World War II. Trotsky explains why only a party fighting to bring workers into its ranks and leadership can steer a communist course. In the process, he defends the materialist and dialectical foundations of Marxism. $17. Also in Spanish.

Labor's Giant Step
The First Twenty Years of the CIO: 1936–55
ART PREIS

The story of the explosive labor struggles and political battles in the 1930s that built the industrial unions. And how those unions became the vanguard of a mass social movement that began transforming US society. $27

50 Years of Covert Operations in the US
Washington's Political Police and the American Working Class
LARRY SEIGLE, FARRELL DOBBS
STEVE CLARK

How class-conscious workers have fought against the drive to build the "national security" state essential to maintaining capitalist rule. $10. Also in Spanish and Farsi.

The Teamster Series
FARRELL DOBBS

Four books on the strikes, organizing drives, and political campaigns that transformed the Teamsters across the Midwest in the 1930s into a militant industrial union movement. Written by Farrell Dobbs, the general organizer of these Teamster battles and leader of the Socialist Workers Party.

A tool for workers seeking to use union power in every workplace and advance the fight for an independent labor party. $16 each, series $50. Also in Spanish. *Teamster Rebellion* is also available in French, Farsi, and Greek.

Trade Unions in the Epoch of Imperialist Decay
LEON TROTSKY, FARRELL DOBBS
KARL MARX

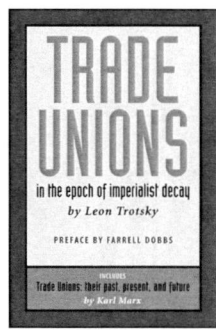

"The trade unions can be really independent of the capitalist state only to the extent that they are conscious of being, in addition, the organs of proletarian revolution." $15

Cosmetics, Fashions, and the Exploitation of Women
JOSEPH HANSEN, EVELYN REED, MARY-ALICE WATERS

How big business reinforces women's second-class status and uses it to rake in profits. Where does women's oppression come from? How has the entry of millions of women into the workforce strengthened the battle for emancipation, still to be won? $12. Also in Spanish, Farsi, and Greek.

Malcolm X Talks to Young People

"The young generation of whites, Blacks, browns, whatever else—you're living at a time of revolution," said Malcolm in 1964. "And I for one will join with anyone, I don't care what color you are, as long as you want to change this miserable condition that exists on this earth." Four talks and an interview in the last months of Malcolm's life. $12. Also in Spanish, French, Farsi, and Greek.

Thomas Sankara Speaks
The Burkina Faso Revolution, 1983–87

Under Sankara's guidance, Burkina Faso's revolutionary government led peasants, workers, women, and youth to expand literacy; to sink wells, plant trees, erect housing; to combat women's oppression; to carry out land reform; to join others worldwide to free themselves from the imperialist yoke. $20. Also in French.

FBI on Trial
The Victory in the Socialist Workers Party Suit against Government Spying
MARGARET JAYKO

The record of a historic victory in the fight for political rights, including the 1986 federal court ruling against government spying and excerpts from trial testimony by SWP leaders Farrell Dobbs and Jack Barnes. $17

Letters from Prison
A Revolutionary Party Prepares for Post–WWII Labor Battles
JAMES P. CANNON

The prison letters of a communist leader, jailed for his party's opposition to the US imperialist war effort in World War II. Cannon discusses organizing a revolutionary party in wartime and preparing its postwar political course. $20

Maurice Bishop Speaks
The Grenada Revolution and Its Overthrow, 1979–83

The triumph of the 1979 revolution in the Caribbean island of Grenada under the leadership of Maurice Bishop gave hope to millions throughout the Americas. Invaluable lessons from the workers and farmers government destroyed by a Stalinist-led counterrevolution in 1983. $20

Anti-Dühring and Dialectics of Nature
FREDERICK ENGELS

Anti-Dühring rebuts the dogma of a reformist professor, whose backers, Engels says, sought "to spread this doctrine in a popular form among workers" and turn the working-class party in Germany into a "little sect." Bolshevik leader V.I. Lenin called it "a handbook for every class-conscious worker" aiming to uproot exploitation and oppression.

A companion work, *Dialectics of Nature*, explains the interconnection between natural science and the evolution of human society.

Both are in *Marx and Engels Collected Works*, vol. 25, $35.

The Origin of the Family, Private Property, and the State
FREDERICK ENGELS

The emergence of class-divided society gave rise to repressive state bodies and the oppression of women to enable the ruling classes to pass along wealth and privilege. Engels discusses the consequences for working people of these class institutions—from their ancient forms to their modern versions. $15. Also in Spanish and Farsi.

Pathfinder Press **accessible ebooks** for the blind, those with low vision, or other challenges reading print books

For a list of current accessible titles, go to: pathfinderpress.com/collections/books-for-the-blind.

Visit Bookshare.org for information on how to sign up.

WWW.PATHFINDERPRESS.COM

CUBA'S SOCIALIST REVOLUTION

October 1962
The 'Missile' Crisis as Seen from Cuba
TOMÁS DIEZ ACOSTA

In October 1962 Washington pushed the world to the edge of nuclear war. Here the full story of that historic moment is told from the perspective of the Cuban people, whose determination to defend their sovereignty and their socialist revolution blocked US plans for a devastating military assault. $17

Red Zone
Cuba and the Battle against Ebola in West Africa
ENRIQUE UBIETA GÓMEZ

When three African countries were hit in 2014–15 by the Ebola epidemic, Cuba's revolutionary government sent what no other country even pretended to provide: more than 250 volunteer doctors, nurses, and other medical workers. This firsthand account of their actions shows the kind of men and women only a socialist revolution can produce. $17. Also in Spanish and French.

The First and Second Declarations of Havana

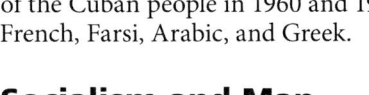

Nowhere are the questions of revolutionary strategy that today confront men and women on the front lines of struggles in the Americas addressed with greater truthfulness and clarity than in these uncompromising indictments of imperialist plunder and "the exploitation of man by man." Adopted by million-strong assemblies of the Cuban people in 1960 and 1962. $10. Also in Spanish, French, Farsi, Arabic, and Greek.

Socialism and Man in Cuba
ERNESTO CHE GUEVARA
FIDEL CASTRO

"Man truly reaches his full human condition when he produces without being compelled by physical necessity to sell himself as a commodity," wrote Guevara in 1965. $5. Also in Spanish, French, Farsi, and Greek.

Our History Is Still Being Written
The Story of Three Chinese Cuban Generals in the Cuban Revolution
ARMANDO CHOY, GUSTAVO CHUI
MOISÉS SÍO WONG
MARY-ALICE WATERS

"What was the key measure to uproot discrimination against Chinese and blacks in Cuba? It was the socialist revolution itself." New edition sheds light on Chinese Cubans' involvement in Cuba's internationalist course, including in Africa and Latin America. $15. Also in Spanish, French, Farsi, Greek, and Chinese.

Cuba and Angola:
The War for Freedom
HARRY VILLEGAS ("POMBO")

The story of Cuba's unparalleled contribution to the fight to free Africa from the scourge of apartheid. And how, in the doing, Cuba's socialist revolution was strengthened. $10. Also in Spanish, Farsi, and Greek.

Che Guevara Talks to Young People

Guevara challenges the youth of Cuba and the world to work. To become disciplined. To join the vanguard on the front lines of struggles, small and large. To become a different kind of human being as they fight together with working people of all lands to transform the world. $12. Also in Spanish and Greek.

Che Guevara:
Economics and Politics in the Transition to Socialism
CARLOS TABLADA

Quoting extensively from Guevara's writings and speeches on building socialism, this book presents the interrelationship of the market, economic planning, material incentives, and voluntary work. Guevara shows why profit and other capitalist categories cannot be yardsticks for progress in the transition to socialism. $17. Also in Spanish, French, and Greek.